Media in Ireland: The Search for Ethical Journalism

MEDIA IN IRELAND

THE SEARCH FOR ETHICAL JOURNALISM

EDITED BY

Damien Kiberd

OPEN AIR

Set in Janson for
OPEN AIR
an imprint of Four Courts Press
Fumbally Lane, Dublin 8, Ireland
e-mail: info@four-courts-press.ie
and in North America for
Four Courts Press, c/o ISBS,
5804 N.E. Hassalo Street, Portland
Oregon 97213, USA

A catalogue record for this title
is available from the British Library

ISBN 1-85182-509-6

Printed in Ireland
by Colour Books Ltd, Dublin

Contents

Notes on Contributors

Claude-Jean Bertrand, Professor at the French Press Institute in Paris, specializes in the study of 'world media' and 'media ethics'. He serves on the board of a number of international media journals and has been Visiting Professor at Syracuse University's School of Journalism. His recent book on media ethics (*La Déontologie des Médias*, Presses Universitaires de France, 1997) will be published shortly by Transaction Books, Rutgers, New Jersey, under the title *Media Ethics and Accountability Systems*.

Conor Brady is Editor of the *Irish Times*. He is chairman of the World Editors' Forum and a board member of the World Newspapers Association (FIEJ).

Seán Duignan presents *The Week in Politics* on RTE Network 2 TV. A former Political Correspondent with RTE, he has detailed his experiences as Government Press Secretary in the book *One Spin on the Merry-Go-Round* (1995).

Robert Healy was Executive Editor of the *Boston Globe*, and its Washington Bureau Chief for many years. His syndicated column appeared in 90 newspapers throughout the US and his reports led to the first Pulitzer Gold Medal award for his newspaper. He lectured at Harvard University's Institute of Politics for eight years.

William Hunt is an American financial consultant, now based in Ireland, who has worked in Greece and the Middle East.

Damien Kiberd is Editor of the *Sunday Business Post*.

Robert Pinker is a member of the British Press Complaints Commission and its Privacy Commissioner. He was Professor of Social Administration at the London School of Economics until 1996 and is now Professor Emeritus.

Andy Pollak is Education Correspondent of the *Irish Times*. His father came to Northern Ireland as a refugee from Czechoslovakia in 1948.

Brendan Purcell is a Lecturer in the Philosophy Department at University College Dublin and a priest of the Dublin diocese. He has a special interest in Eric Voegelin, a 20th-century political philosopher, and recently published *The Drama of Humanity: Towards a Philosophy of Humanity in History* (1996).

Klaus Schönbach is Professor of General Communications Science at the University of Amsterdam. At the time of the conference he was Professor of Mass Communication and Director of the Department of Journalism and Communication Research at the University of Music and Theatre in Hanover, Germany. He has been a Visiting Professor at Cleveland State University, Indiana University and San Jose State University. He has published widely in English and German.

Preface

DAMIEN KIBERD

S ome journalists like to refer to their occupation as a trade. Others describe it as a profession. All would, however, agree that they should aspire to the highest possible professional standards.

This book is in many ways about the achievement of such professionalism. Unlike doctors or lawyers, journalists do not have powerful regulatory bodies such as the Medical Council or the Bar Council to monitor the achievement of acceptable levels of professionalism, or to assess ethical problems as they arise. Most of Irish journalism is self-regulating, and many Irish journalists and editors would prefer that it should remain so.

Yet there is an ongoing debate about standards in the Irish and international media, a debate which provokes quite enormous interest.

The following essays, presented at the Seventh Cleraun Media Conference (see p. 105), form a part of that debate. They are written by working journalists and editors, by those involved in the professional training of journalists, by those who have taken time to examine ethical considerations affecting journalists and by those who have sought to apply standards to journalists' work.

Together they present a picture of, perhaps inevitable, imperfection. Two essays (Pollak and Schönbach) deal with an issue of great contemporary importance: the influence of the mass media on public and official attitudes to immigrants. Pollak's carefully researched analysis of the Irish media's response to relatively modest levels of inward migration must cause great concern, for parts of the media may have provoked suspicion and animosity among people of previously open minds whose own historic experience should have promoted understanding of the problems encountered by economic migrants and refugees. Schönbach recounts how even factual reportage of a potentially fraught situation may lead to harmful effects.

Three other essays (Bertrand, Pinker and Healy) examine the methods whereby the media industry may become more accountable. Bertrand sees a compelling role for the managers and owners of media businesses in establishing media accountability systems. Pinker speaks of his experience of the British Press Complaints Commission, an honest if imperfect attempt to reconcile the competing needs to vindicate simultaneously the right to privacy, the right to freedom of expression and the public interest. Healy examines the role of the newspaper ombudsman, and suggests that journalists can be quick learners when the price of mistaken judgements is sufficiently high.

In an important contribution, Brady examines the suffocating role played by very outmoded laws of libel and defamation in Ireland. He explains how, paradoxically, these laws inhibit editors and journalists from offering immediate and suitable redress to those wronged by newspapers or broadcasting organizations. Frequently these laws do not make the media accountable in any real sense: and they prevent speedy resolution of problems as they arise.

The opening essay (Purcell) of this collection examines more fundamental philosophical issues affecting journalists. In a society where common discourse is afflicted by growing levels of ingrained falsehood, how does a working journalist benchmark his or her work? The closing essay (Duignan) offers a view from the other side of the fence, as the author recounts his experiences as a well-meaning manipulator of the media.

Though the standard of professional and academic training available to journalists has improved greatly in recent years, it is still unclear to those who have studied these issues whether or not a school or college can teach working journalists a system of professional ethics. In a sense, working journalists develop a workable system of ethics through their work, by taking correct decisions every day in a constantly changing environment. The highly competitive nature of the media industry will mean that there are constant pressures to abandon ethical concepts and practices. These pressures will exert themselves against a background in which there has been a palpable 'dumbing-down', in significant areas of the media. Sometimes the lowering of standards is described as a 'pushing out of barriers'. It is, equally, hard to see where the process will end. What may become apparent over time is that those parts of the media which embrace strong systems of internal and external accountability become more highly valued by readers, listeners and viewers.

Introduction

WILLIAM HUNT

The eight chapters of this book are contributed by individuals whose roles range from working journalist to academic, from regulator to editor. Together they provide an expert assessment of the most important issues facing the Irish media at the present, and not only raise concerns with current ethical standards within the media, but show what steps are being taken, and what steps might be taken, to assure that public confidence in the industry's professional standards is retained. They begin with **Brendan Purcell**'s discussion of the ethical dimension of journalism, which—in tracing the present-day ethic to its Socratic roots—demonstrates that the journalist's professional ethics have a fundamental philosophical basis, and are not merely the by-laws of a trade association.

Dr Purcell suggests a powerful model for assessing the ethical standards applied in the media industry: he equates the one-sided conversation the media carries on with its audience to the ordinary interaction each of us has with acquaintances and friends, and proposes that the media's professional ethics must, at the least, meet the moral standard each of us would apply to his own daily conversations. While conversation largely consists of friendly if empty exchanges on trivial topics, jokes, entertainment—what Dr Purcell would term 'pragmatic'—when we *do* speak of something important it is with the intention of informing our listeners, not misinforming them.

This model of an ordinary conversation makes it clearer that journalistic ethics are a fundamental part of the journalist's profession. Individuals do not have *rules* for conversations. There is instead an implicit assumption of good faith: that the speaker believes what he is saying, and is saying it because he feels that it is in the interest of the listener to hear it. The same good faith intention on the part of the media is assumed, but is further reinforced by its code of ethics.

Dr Purcell reminds us that this code—the list of those things that a journalist must do and those he must not—does not in itself *constitute* the journalist's ethic. The list defines the ethic only in the sense that the outline on a map defines a nation: the people and places within the line probably belong to that country, and most of the people and places outside do not. There will necessarily be exceptions, even on the technical point of who is carrying the country's passport and who is carrying that of another; but at best the map outline can deal only with the legalistic question of what the *country* comprises: the *nation*—a larger, grander, and far more abstract idea—defines itself. While what is expected of a journalist is that he share the equivalent of the spirit of a nation, there are practical reasons why his specific ethics are more like the constitution of a country.

The explicit rules set for ethical journalism serve three separate purposes. Firstly, they provide guidance for the individual journalist faced with a particularly hard case, where his fundamental motivation leaves him balanced between alternatives; he knows that the specific formulation of his profession's ethic has served others before him in similar circumstances, and that he may rely on them. Secondly, they permit both the public and fellow professionals to impeach the actions of journalists who have failed in their obligations; for this purpose an explicit, even if approximate, formulation of the underlying ethic is needed—in much the same way that our court system can deal only with actions that are illegal, not those that are immoral. Finally, a profession must take a longer and broader view than any individual can. Some portions of the ethic therefore establish that individual journalists must sometimes make sacrifices—accept constraints on their desire to inform the public by, for example, refusing to use material that has been obtained dishonestly—in order that the profession as a whole, and over time, may continue to do so more effectively.

The rules are necessary, but—more importantly—professional ethics must also be internalized. We do not want our GP to tell us we have a serious medical problem that we do not have just in order to schedule us into his surgery once a week for the next few months, at £20 a visit. Still less do we want him to fail to tell us of his early diagnosis of a disease because it will be more profitable for him to treat once it has had more time to develop. Neither is it enough that he simply not do these things. We want him to refrain from doing them not because he might be found out and struck off the register—but because he does not *want* to do them. We expect him to be motivated, in his professional dealings with us, by the desire to promote our health and well-being. His Hippocratic Oath, the specifics of the medical ethics to which his colleagues hold him accountable, should have no part in his day-to-day dealings with patients. A physician should have so internalized his objective of serving his patients that he should need to consider explicitly the ethics of his profession only in the rarest of cases, where some delicate balance between the good and the harm he might do by following a certain course—or between two harms—is not easily resolved by instinct alone.

The public expects the same of journalists: personal commitment to the underlying ethic of their profession. If we admire a journalist with professional integrity, what we have noted is not that he scrupulously follows the rules of his craft, but that he has *integrated* the professional, commercial and ethical demands of journalism into a whole from which the ethical component is inseparable.

It is ethics that make journalism a profession. How many of us would be comfortable describing the men and women who worked in the news media in Eastern Europe prior to glasnost and the collapse of the Soviet system *as journalists*? Not many—because we mean by the word something different from merely someone who works in a particular industry in a specific type of job. They must also be members of a profession that could not have functioned, because of its basic ethics, in any member of the Warsaw Pact before this decade. Karl Marx himself said that all would be lost if journalism ever came to be a mere trade; that the political system established in his name should have made it one with such thoroughness goes beyond irony. We could accept 'journalist' as the appropriate word for the editor of *Pravda* in 1975 with much less discomfort than we could accept 'physician' for Josef Mengele, but the difference is only one of degree. 'Unethical journalist' is a contradiction in terms. Adherence to the underlying ethic of journalism is as much a part of being a journalist as the honouring of the Hippocratic Oath is an essential part of being a physician: an unethical journalist or unethical medical doctor is not a member of *any* profession—he is merely a fraud waiting to be found out, whether or not he has so far managed to live by his explicit professional rules.

A number of the chapters following Dr Purcell's suggest that the issue of media ethics is not a hypothetical one, that there may be a fundamental problem that the industry, and the public, should address. Andy Pollak provides examples of the harm that can be done when journalists fail to follow scrupulously their ethical code. More alarmingly, Klaus Schönbach shows that great damage can also result when the explicit code *is* followed, but the intent of it ignored—in other words, when journalists fail to internalize their ethic—and proposes a refinement that would prevent this. Seán Duignan demonstrates that 'leaking', in which a journalist must necessarily misrepresent to a degree the source of reported material, has become a firmly established practice upon which both politicians and journalists increasingly depend. Furthermore, the growing attention being paid within the industry to 'media accountability systems' is reflected not only in Prof. Bertrand's overview of this subject, but in the individual chapters devoted to specific mechanisms: Conor Brady on libel law, Robert Pinker on the British Press Complaints Commission, and Robert Healy on ombudsmen. We must ask ourselves why increasing interest is being attracted to methods for *enforcing* adherence to an ethic that ought, not only in an ideal world but in a merely decent one, to be so far internalized by media professionals as to justify scant attention even within the profession, let alone engage the interest of the public.

While many chapters in this book may suggest that there are problems, they also, if only indirectly, point to a possible solution. Happily, it is a solution entirely in the power of the media to implement: by reporting more fully on itself.

Journalists are often accused of self-absorption, of engaging in self-referential games with each other, of so losing themselves in their profession that they are in danger of also losing contact both with the world they are supposed to be reporting on and the audience they are supposed to be reporting it to. The media's desire not to further support this accusation, which is not totally unfounded but is certainly greatly exaggerated, is perhaps the principal reason for their reluctance to report on an aspect of our world that has not received coverage in anything like proportion to its importance: the media itself. There are other reasons. A journalist or newspaper, say, would be rightly concerned that a negative report on a rival could be motivated by self-interest rather than by the desire to inform, and therefore contrary to accepted journalistic ethics. Conversely, a favourable report would presumably benefit a rival—a high price for an enterprise, or an individual, to pay in an intensely competitive market. Neither can we forget that journalism is a small world. The journalists within any community form a village within a village; however large the city, its journalists have no more pubs than any other village does, and if they are to continue to drink together, the decencies must be observed.

Whatever the reason for it, the reluctance is there. The media keep their public reasonably well informed of the economic realities facing other institutions, but not those facing the media. How many of the public understand the importance of advertising revenue to their newspapers, and know of the great differences among them in their reliance on this income source? The media keep their public informed of the operation of the laws of this country and actively campaign against those that appear harmful to the common good, but not if they affect the media. How many readers, viewers or listeners are aware of the extent to which the reporting of the news, on which they must rely to intelligently exercise their democratic rights, is constrained by Ireland's singularly ferocious libel laws? The media, both specialized and generalist, provide consumers with information on most of the products they buy, praising the best value and highest quality, warning of special dangers—but not those of the products of the media itself. How many of us are aware of the inherent advantages and disadvantages of each different medium in presenting us with various categories of information, or how the professionals view the individual strengths and weaknesses of the particular newspaper we choose to read, network we choose to watch or station we choose to listen to?

None of the following chapters directly addresses the question of whether the media gives enough attention to its own role in the process of informing us on the workings of the world we live in. Each assesses a different aspect of the media's performance from the perspective of authors playing diverse roles. Each raises different questions, identifies different potential problems and suggests different solutions. Many of the authors themselves might not, in fact, agree that fuller reporting to the public on the media was at all desirable. It is therefore particularly interesting to read the chapters with this thought in the back of one's mind: would the media better serve its public if the *media itself* were to feature more explicitly in its own coverage of the institutions that govern our lives? Most chapters, in addition to authoritative comment on their specific subject matter, give their own insight into this more general topic.

Andy Pollak examines aspects of the media coverage of issues related to those seeking political asylum here in Ireland. He focuses particularly on newspaper reporting from the spring of 1997 onward, and finds it in many respects unsatisfactory. Of his cases, perhaps the most startling is that of the phantom Romanian and Somali rapists, in which a report was printed, citing 'Gardaí' and 'top Garda sources', as warning all women to stay away from refugees because of a plague of sexual attacks being carried out in parts of Dublin. There were undoubtedly some red faces in D'Olier Street the morning the report was run, since Mr Pollak's own paper, the *Irish Times*, had been completely ignorant of these events and carried not a word of them. If the faces were still red that afternoon, it would not have been from embarrassment. They had tracked down the sole source for this headline story: an individual Garda who was unable to provide any hard evidence that any such attack, let alone a series of them, had occurred. The reporting by the *Irish Times*'s rival had been manifestly inaccurate—although we should possibly be also alarmed by the thought that if there had been *two* confused Gardaí instead of only one, the report would have been technically accurate, and only misleading. A question we should ask ourselves is: why is it that the thousands of readers of this book are learning about this more so long after the event, rather than the hundreds of thousands of readers of Mr Pollak's paper learning about it the next day? Was it not important for *Irish Times* readers to know that hundreds of thousands of their fellow citizens were going about their business convinced that these phantom attacks had actually occurred, forming general views on the refugee issue partly on the basis of them, and then trying—perhaps successfully—to persuade the *Irish Times*'s own readers of their validity? The media's creation of this urban legend—one seriously prejudicial to refugees—was itself a legitimate news story, yet was not reported as such: an inexplicable pause in the *Irish Times*'s 'conversation' with its readers on the refugee issue.

In contrast, **Klaus Schönbach**'s review of media treatment of the refugee issue in Germany demonstrates that, even where the media does adhere strictly to its ethic of accuracy, the result can be creation in the public mind, from correct details, of an impression that incorrectly identifies the underlying issues and available options. He shows how a stream of reports—each scrupulously accurate, none in any way inflammatory, and some actually very amusing—could have contributed to an atmosphere in which attacks on foreign workers and refugees came to be seen by some as a solution to a problem, rather than as a problem in themselves. Further, he concludes that the reporting of each cycle of attacks could have contributed to prolonging rather than ending them. Prof. Schönbach proposes that the media adopt a new ethic, which would require journalists to anticipate the effect of their reporting on the public and which, had it been practised, would have prevented many of these attacks and the sense of frustration that gave rise to them. He is confident that the public would willingly consent to this new ethic. From the developments he describes, however, one could also conclude that—even without these greater responsibilities being accepted by all journalists—contemporary assessment in the German media of where this sort of reporting was leading could have fixed the public's attention on the dangers of the course the media had taken, and possibly prevented further media encouragement to racial attacks. Dr Purcell's 'conversation' model establishes that to provide correct information without the intent to inform is no more ethical than providing incorrect information; both show contempt for the public—and this appears to have been what happened in this case.

Claude-Jean Bertrand advocates a greater role for the owners in assuring that the media they control serve their publics well. This is a controversial view; many, including Prof. Bertrand himself until recently, felt that this was better left to the professionals, and that the owners should step back from their responsibility. He cites many cases, however, of high-quality and correspondingly influential newspapers having been deliberately created or maintained by their owners, and notes that this can never be done without at least their strong support. He assesses dozens of Media Accountability Systems (MAS)—ranging from letters-to-the-editor pages open to criticism of the newspaper itself, to local or regional media councils and journalism reviews—and finds that they constitute methods of quality control, which *should* be equally welcomed by the public, journalists, management and owners alike. His research, however, suggests that the implementation of MAS's is disappointingly slow in almost all parts of the world, a puzzling phenomenon since in virtually all other industries quality control is essential to continued profitability. The difference in the media industry may well be the public's ignorance of its product. When a consumer buys a car that doesn't work, he *knows*—but how many consumers know whether their newspaper or television station 'works'? Only the media can provide the 'product information' that would elevate public demand for quality control to a level that would make it commercially necessary to media providers—nowhere else do we find the knowledge to assess, the skill to describe and the machinery to disseminate this information.

Conor Brady surveys the background and effects of Irish publishing law, and the efforts being made by the media both to operate within and to amend one of the most daunting libel-law regimes anywhere in the developed world. He notes that one of the perverse effects of the current, extremely old system is that a newspaper that knows it has published a mistaken and negative report is often prevented from immediately correcting its mistake because the correction would be far more likely to provoke an expensive lawsuit than would the original libel. Ironically, then, our libel laws prevent us from hearing not only negative things about prominent people that in most other countries would be safely in the public domain, but positive ones as well. Mr Brady outlines the alternative methods of redress that might otherwise be open to those who feel they have been unfairly treated in the media—methods that would be accessible to those unable to finance legal action as well as to the better-off—and finds most of them inoperable under current legal conditions. One exception is the Readers' Representative, of which he details the *Irish Times*'s experience. He also recounts the twelve-year campaign by the Irish media to update the law. Unsurprisingly—since politicians are the principal beneficiaries of the current system, both financially and in terms of their ability to control what the public learn of their activities—there has been no progress whatsoever. Mr Brady notes the irony inherent in the 1994 draft bill, reflecting the 1991 findings of the Law Reform Commission, being presented to Albert Reynolds for action. Missing from Mr Brady's account—missing not because he neglects to mention it, but because it didn't happen—is the story of the media's concerted attempt to inform the public of the issue, and to enlist their support in obliging our politicians to live, if not in the current decade, at least in this century, while there is some of it left. There would have been an element of self-interest in such a campaign, but this should not have prevented it. Reform of our libel laws is much more in the public's interest than in the interest of any individual media organization: had the 1994 draft bill been debated and passed by the Oireachtas, Mr Brady would not have sold any more newspapers; he would merely have been able to print more, and more complete, news in those he did sell.

Robert Pinker describes the situation faced by the British Press Complaints Commission in its efforts to balance the rights of free expression, of privacy and of access to the information needed by the public to make effective and democratic decisions. He assesses both the new Code of Practice under which British newspapers operate and the current arguments on the status of the Commission, whether it is or is not a public authority, and the potential implications of this. As Prof. Pinker details the workings of the Commission, those who at some time have had reason for complaint against an Irish newspaper may develop a sense of envy—and should recall that such a voluntary organization is a practical impossibility in the Irish legal context portrayed by Conor Brady.

Robert Healy's direct, and positive, experience with the *Boston Globe*'s ombudsman and his observations on the mixed success of the role at other newspapers confirm Prof. Bertrand's belief that the commitment of owners and their representatives is necessary for an accountability/quality control system to work well. The ombudsman's job—fielding public complaints, following his own suspicions and investigating within his newspaper possible failures in its coverage, then publishing a column detailing his conclusions—can only be welcome, and possibly can only even work, in an environment where all are committed to maintaining the highest standards of journalism and are willing that the public be made aware immediately when performance falls short. It is a far from common solution. Only a small percentage of American media companies, and none here, have adopted ombudsmen. Where they do exist, the workings of the media and the media's performance *do* become news. Ironically, even this can result in the public's gaining a distorted picture of the performance of the media, since it is those journals with the highest standards and which give their ombudsmen the greatest authority that may *appear*, from the comments of the ombudsmen, to be doing the worst jobs. If, instead, the 'unwritten law', under which the 'press ignores the errors and misrepresentations, the lies and scandals, of … its members' were to be repealed, and the media free to report on itself, then no newspaper would be obliged to employ an ombudsman to make the public aware of its failures to maintain the highest professional and ethical standards: some other newspaper would do it for them.

Seán Duignan, from his perspective as both an experienced journalist and former (and one might say, self-confessed) 'spin-doctor', is especially well placed to assess the growing practice of 'leaking', and to provide significant examples of it from recent Irish politics. His light-hearted tone is deceptive; he is clearly concerned that the practice has established itself as a necessary evil both in Irish politics and Irish journalism—and it is with a touch of pride that he acknowledges his not having been very good at it. We can understand why a journalist would not disdain leaks, and even why sources of them would be actively cultivated: leaks are by their nature both good, startling news stories *and* exclusive. What prospector would continue the backbreaking labour of digging rocks out of a mine that only *might* contain gold when the stream at the foot of the hill is awash with huge nuggets of it?

Of the three separate aspects of the evil of leaking, however, this is probably the most important: that it diverts journalists from that mine—the mine of what politicians *don't* want the public to know—into panning the stream of what they *do* want the public to know. The second evil is that the price of plucking one of these nuggets from the stream is that the journalist must lie about where he found it; he must make it appear that he dug it from the mine. It may, in terms of Dr Purcell's 'conversation' between the media and the public, be only a white lie—but it is a lie nonetheless. One of the ironies of leaking is that this ritual deception never fools the victims of the leak, who know perfectly well what has happened, as Mr Duignan makes clear. Not every member of the public is equally sophisticated, however; many will take the story at face value—as the fruit of investigative reporting, fully sourced and counter-checked—and assume it is further evidence that the media is hard at work on their behalf. The third evil derives from our becoming accustomed to vague descriptions of sources being given in news reports. Even the most knowing among us will only nod sagely at a source's being identified as 'a highly-placed and well-informed source at the Department of Foreign Affairs', and speculate on just which it is of the two people we suspect—without imagining that *this* time it is the cleaner who empties the bins on the top floor. Would the deplorable 'refugee rapist' story described by Andy Pollak have been possible if we had not already been conditioned, through the conventions of leaking, to read 'top Garda sources' to mean something quite different from one individual Garda at a Dublin station? If the public understood what was actually happening they would continue to want the information provided through leaking—it is often important and rarely uninteresting—but they would not accept the degree of misrepresentation inherent in the present method. There is no reason why leaked information could not be preceded by the simple statement that 'someone wants you to know this but doesn't want me to tell you who he or she is'; *that*, after all, is only the truth.

So, is the media keeping up its end of the conversation on the subject of the media itself? It would appear not. The public is less well informed about the media than about any institution of comparable importance. As long as its audience lacks sufficient 'product information' to make them intelligent and demanding consumers, there will be no possibility of generating a commercial demand that the media impose 'quality control' on itself, and there are at present no signs of the alternative—an ethically-motivated campaign from within the profession. If the market ceases to value competence and integrity in its journalists, then these qualities will come to be devalued within the industry, its ethics reduced to a rule book and the professional standing of journalism put in serious doubt. The market can value only what the public can recognise, so it should be in the interests of all in the industry to assure that they have an informed and discriminating audience.

What would Socrates say?
Towards a foundation in media ethics

BRENDAN PURCELL

One of István Örkény's *One Minute Stories*, 'Life should be so simple'[1] seems very relevant to our topic. It goes like this:

1. remove fire extinguisher from bracket
2. open valve
3. approach source of fire
4. extinguish fire
5. close valve
6. replace extinguisher on bracket.

Life should be so simple. But it isn't. So we shouldn't have too many illusions that in a little over half an hour even a zippy job can be done on the foundations of media ethics. But we can move 'towards' a foundation if we clear one thing up. There *isn't* any media ethics, in the sense of some kind of big filing cabinet with Ethics on the outside, containing different files for Law, Medicine, Journalism, and so on, to which ethical principles can be stuck on like labels. Just as the legal and medical professions have got to work out what's right and wrong in the light of their own requirements to serve justice or health, so, I think, have the media, in the light of their requirement to serve the truth. And what I'll suggest here is that as a starting point we could take a fairly basic experience we all have in some way or another—talking to a friend in a pub, at a match, over a meal.

Because what's going on there is the basic raw material of the media, someone honestly communicating to someone else, and the other person communicating to him or her. What can distort and undermine communication, as it can any other aspect of a human relationship, is the desire of the stronger to take advantage over the weaker. Once this happens, we've got the misuse of communication, as a form of verbal violence or trickery, in order to control or instrumentalize the other by the lie.[2]

---

1 In: *One Minute Stories*, tr. Judith Sollosy (Budapest: Corvina, 1997), p. 20. 2 In the light of the extremely useful papers by Mr Andy Pollak (pp. 33-46) and Professor Klaus Schönbach (pp. 47-

'Being forbidden to travel to the West or to choose the kind of work I'll do isn't what bothers me the most. What really gets me down is being lied to so much.'

Chris Hirte was a student at the Humboldt University in what in 1970, was East Berlin, whom I met while on a language course there. He was by no means starry-eyed about the quality of West Berlin TV programmes, yet felt he could filter out what was propaganda from them easily enough. But he experienced a consciously lying DDR media as an attack on his dignity as a human being. As R.D. Laing put it once, 'I'm sure that truth-deprivation can wreak as much havoc ... as vitamin deprivation.'[3]

So all communication can be seen firstly in terms of the communicating person's respect for his or her audience. Secondly, the people receiving the communication have to keep up their end of the conversation by responsibly paying attention to the communicator. And thirdly, there's the resulting community of trust brought about by these actions of respectful talking and listening.[4]

To help to take a closer look at this fairly basic notion of communication, following the Austrian political philosopher, Eric Voegelin,[5] I'd like to refer to genuine truth-sharing as *substantive communication*, its opposite as *disintegrative communication*, and a kind of half-in-half form as *pragmatic communication*.

SUBSTANTIVE COMMUNICATION

In his Seventh Letter, Plato spelt out what he considered was at the heart of true communication between human beings:

> One statement at any rate I can make in regard to all who have written or who may write with a claim to knowledge of the subjects to which I devote myself [i.e. philosophy] ... Such writers can in my opinion have no real acquaintance with the subject. I certainly have composed no

58), I'd like to refer to Eric Voegelin's clarification of the meaning of the lie, which for him can range from: 'the straight lie concerning a fact to the subtler lie of arranging a context in such a manner that the omission of the fact will not be noticed; or from the construction of a system that, by its form suggests its partial view as the whole of reality to its author's refusal to discuss the premises of the system in terms of reality experienced', in *The Collected Works of Eric Voegelin*, vol. 28, eds. Thomas Hollweck & Paul Caringella (Baton Rouge: Louisiana State University Press, 1990), p. 113. **3** *The Facts of Life* (Penguin, London, 1977), p. 136. **4** We could present this schematically as a 'happy circle' of i) communicator's respect for audience; ii) audience's attentive reception; iii) community of truth and of trust. Note 7 below further develops this 'happy circle' of communication. **5** Cf. Eric Voegelin, 'Necessary Moral Bases for Communication in a Democracy', in *Problems of Communication in a Pluralistic Society*, [no editor named] (Milwaukee: Marquette University Press, 1956), pp. 54-68.

work in regard to it, nor shall I ever do so in the future, for there is no way of putting it in words like other studies ... After scrutinizing [philosophical issues] in benevolent disputation by the use of question and answer without jealousy, at last in a flash understanding of each blazes up, and the mind, as it exerts all its powers to the limit of human capacity, is flooded with light.[6]

For Plato, then, communication isn't a matter of dominating or using other people, it's a matter of a shared quest for truth. And his preferred medium for this was the living dialogue, of which his written dialogues were only the record. But there's a price to pay: Socrates' presence in almost all of the dialogues is a reminder that achieving and communicating the truth may be at the cost of opposing socially dominant lies, an opposition that may demand losing one's shirt, if not one's life. And the audience too will have to be prepared to suffer if it wants to take on the consequences of truth over against the lie. That's why we can speak of genuine dialogue as substantive communication, a communication of the substance of our humanity leading to what Plato speaks of in the *Gorgias* (508a) as *koinonia* or communion.

What comes over from the *Gorgias* is that Socrates is only interested in helping his audience arrive for themselves at the truth. Socrates also invites them to help him to get beyond any intellectual blocks or errors he may be making himself, showing his awareness that the work of communication is a two-way affair.

On the one hand, then, there's what, for want of a better term, we can call 'communication from above,' which is the side of communication initiated by the media professionals. As an example, let me select from some pieces Michael Kelly wrote for the *Washington Post*.

In 'I Believe' (4 February 1998) he wrote:

> I believe the president. I have always believed him. I believed him when he said he had never been drafted in the Vietnam War and I believed him when he said he had forgotten to mention that he had been drafted in the Vietnam War...I believe Paula Jones is a cheap tramp who was asking for it. I believe Kathleen Willey is a cheap tramp who was asking for it. I believe Monica Lewinsky is a cheap tramp who was asking for it...I believe the instructions Lewinsky gave Tripp informing her on how to properly perjure herself in the Willey matter simply wrote themselves. I believe that the *Washington Post*, the *Los Angeles Times*, the *New York Times*, *Newsweek*, *Time*, *US News and World Report*, ABC, CBS,

---

6 Cf. *The Collected Dialogues of Plato*, eds. Edith Hamilton and Huntington Cairns (Princeton: Princeton University Press, 1971), pp. 1588f, 1591.

NBC, CNN, PBS and NPR are all part of a vast right-wing conspiracy. Especially NPR.

And, from the article Kelly wrote a week later, 'Making Liars of Us All' (11 February 1998):

> Assume for the sake of crazy, far-fetched argument that President Clinton is lying about Monica Lewinsky. The line from the president's increasingly cornered defenders is that this doesn't matter...No. The Lewinsky matter is not about the minor and personal question of whatever an individual does in pursuit of happiness behind closed doors...It is about the largest, most central and most public of questions: whether we demand that the president obey the law, whether we accept that the president lies to us...[I]t is this fomenting of corruption that is the great problem with Clinton...The problem with Clinton is not only that he lies; it is that he makes liars out of everybody else. The problem is not only that his moral standards are low; it is that he requires that everybody else lower theirs to meet his. By the time he is finished, so too will be the quaint idea of a higher ground in politics.

Finally, 'Would You Believe He's a Victim?' (18 February 1998):

> [Kelly responds to an Arkansas journalist defending Clinton, who had said: 'If you take someone like the president, who a lot of women would find attractive if he came to fix their garbage disposal, and you make him the President of the United States, the Alpha male of the United States of America, and you sexualize his image with a lot of smears and false accusations so that people think he's Tom Jones or Rod Stewart, then a certain irreducible number of women are going to act batty around him.'] The poor man. The poor victim. My God, how he must have suffered. Stalked through the halls of his own home, and nowhere to turn for protection. Nothing standing between him and a 21-year-old stalker...Nothing except for his wife, his chief of staff, his deputy chief of staff, his secretary, his personal assistant, his special assistants, his National Security Council, his Marine guard, three dozen or so Secret Service agents and the Joint Chiefs of Staff. What's a President to do with a stalker but give her gifts, find her a lawyer and advance her career?

What I find in journalism of this quality is an appeal to my own sense of truth and of justice. Michael Kelly is asking his readers to ask themselves what a democracy is about, what citizenship is about. Even when perhaps a majority of those readers, and the editorial line of the paper printing his articles, have tended to support the president through thick and thin.

In response, there's 'communication from below,' which is the audience's reply to the communication from above. I'd suggest that without that response, in the minds and hearts of his readers, Kelly's journalism has no effect whatever. Because communication 'from above' is intrinsically related to communication 'from below.' Not only as responding to it, but also, very often, as providing the very basis for journalism in the first place. If Kelly didn't know that there were at least potential democrats out there, people who care to maintain a democracy, something he knows both from conversation and ordinary experience, he wouldn't write those articles in the first place.

So, what's going on in the interaction between the two cycles of communication, from above and from below, is a shared contribution to the substance of our common humanity.[7]

PRAGMATIC COMMUNICATION

SIAMESE TWIN
SLAYS BROTHER
IN BUNGLED
SUICIDE BID!!

BLUE
BRUTON
BOOBS
IN TWINK
PRANK!!

In our humdrum days often the nearest thing to poetry are the tabloid headlines, a kind of haiku form with strict limits of expression and concision. So let's not complain about tabloid coverage as such. Most media communication is in the area of what used to be called morally neutral—it's got to do with undemanding information regarding everyday matters. This undemanding information includes political and legal information, commercial and

---

[7] That is to say, there is a mutual intersection of i) communicating; ii) assimilating; iii) community- building, with 'happy circles' of communication being initiated both 'from above' and 'from below.' Professor Claude-Jean Bertrand's paper (pp. 59-68), with among other things, its list of Media Accountability Systems, opened this author's eyes to the enormous diversity of expressions of 'communication from below'. There's a fuller account in his *La Déontologie des Médias* (PUF): Paris, 1997, pp. 83-103.

sports news, advertising—overt or concealed—gossip about entertainment and other figures, popular entertainment and so on. While there's nothing wrong with most of this in itself—it probably accounts for three quarters of what goes on in the media—there is a danger that it can slide over into what we'll be calling intoxicant communication.

This danger, quite apart from any question regarding content, propriety or whatever, comes from at least two areas. There's the danger to the media operatives of trivializing themselves, when they confuse the partial or pseudo-reality of their public self-presentation with who they really are.[8] That danger becomes most visible in their products, the media personalities who sell media coverage, with their acute loss of capacity to differentiate their media personae from themselves. Let's call such media personalities 'soul-bytes'.[9] And there's the danger of trivializing their audience. Karl Kraus had already spoken about the effect on an audience habituated to trivialization, in his *Last Days of Mankind*:

> Were not all the realms of imagination evacuated, when that manifesto proclaimed the War to the inhabited earth? In the end was the word. Normally the one who kills the spirit only gives birth to that deed. Weaklings become strong, in order to bring us under the wheel of progress. And it's they, and they alone, who've made that possible, who betrayed the world with their prostitution. Not that the Press got the machines of death going—but that they hollowed out our hearts, so that we couldn't imagine anymore how things were: that is their war-guilt![10]

Let's examine a bit more fully this loss of a sense of self accompanying self-amplification through media, both in journalists and in 'newsmakers' or 'soul-bytes.' Dostoevsky's *The Double* [1846][11] is a penetrating treatment of Mr Golyadkin, a pathetic minor functionary. Golyadkin works in the human desert of a mid-19th century St Petersburg focused on the externals of social position, and utterly indifferent to the uniqueness of each person. In this icily courteous bureaucracy, each de-individualized cog is replaceable by another. Golyadkin, in an anguished search for at least one human being with whom he can relate and experience his own identity, feels constrained to construct an imaginary 'double' and ever narrower 'worlds' around himself, none of

---

8 Paul H. Weaver's *News and the Culture of Lying: How Journalism Really Works* (New York: Free Press, 1994), asks, 'Why do reporters accommodate themselves so comfortably to the requirements of the genre and the pressures of bosses and newsmakers?…Because they have a weak sense of self and a correspondingly strong need for the validation of others, especially powerful others. In other words, we are courtiers…' (p. 148). (Weaver was a writer and editor for *Fortune* magazine.) 9 Chapter 4 of *News and the Culture of Lying* is entitled 'Wayward Heroes.' Its opening line is: 'Newsmakers almost always accept the news story's invitation to posture and lie' (p. 87). 10 Karl Kraus, *Die letzten Tage der Menschheit*, II, Munich: DTV, 1975, p. 230. 11 Easily available from Penguin, 1972, in Jessie Coulson's excellent translation.

which satisfies his inner need for relationship with others. Due to the inevitable friction with the real world, his second reality shatters into smaller and smaller 'worlds.' Golyadkin's 'double' at first 'betrays' him, then disintegrates into an infinite number of temporary 'doubles.' Finally, his imagination can no longer construct further, smaller 'worlds' immunized from the anxiety induced by reality. His ability even to manipulate his own inner fantasy world has broken down. Odd as Golyadkin seems, the entertainment and political worlds continually produce characters whose incapacity to relate to a real world of persons results in fantastic second realities which ultimately evaporate, sometimes with tragic results. The scotoma which results from what Voegelin has spoken of as 'a peculiar compound of insight and intellectual dishonesty,' or 'honest dishonesty,' is the construction of an imaginary world 'which will confirm the self in its pretense of reality ... a Second Reality ... to screen the First Reality of common experience from his view.'[12] There are similarities between the 2nd Self/2nd Reality of someone suffering from schizophrenia,[13] and the 2nd Self/2nd Reality of the person averting himself from truth. And while I'm not trying to make capital from the death of Princess Diana, at least some of these stages may be seen as applicable to her:

Stage 1:   Presentation to public of 2nd self or media personality
Stage 2:   Beginning of domination of 1st self by 2nd self
Stage 3:   Complete loss of control by 1st self to 2nd self
Stage 4:   More or less complete disintegration of personality.

Why should a media presenter, or whoever allows themselves to be presented by the media, slide into such a dangerous loss of control? Pascal offered his notion of *divertissement*, of a fundamental lack of seriousness with regard to the attainment and expression of difficult truth, as the debased social context which welcomes pragmatic communication:

We are not satisfied with the life we have in ourselves and our own being. We want to live an imaginary life in the eyes of others, and so we try to make an impression. We strive constantly to embellish and preserve our imaginary being, and neglect the real one.[14]

This 'aversion from the truth',[15] easily slides from self-deception into hatred of truth, whether that truth originates in self or others:

It conceives a deadly hatred for the truth which rebukes it and convicts it of its faults. It would like to do away with this truth, but not being

12 *The Collected Works of Eric Voegelin*, vol. 28, eds. Thomas Hollweck & Paul Caringella (Baton Rouge: Louisiana State University Press, 1990), pp. 112, 115.   13 Cf. Silvano Arieti's four stages of schizophrenic contraction in his *Interpretation of Schizophrenia* (New York: Robert Brunner, 1955), pp. 321-78.   14 *Pensées* (London: Penguin, 1983), p. 270.   15 Ibid., p. 349.

able to destroy it as such, it destroys it, as best it can, in the conscious-
ness of itself and others; that is, it takes every care to hide its faults both
from itself and others, and cannot bear to have them pointed out or
noticed.[16]

However, journalists and their willing/unwilling accomplices, the 'soul-
bytes,' aren't the only ones who may want, in T.S. Eliot's phrase, to be 'dis-
tracted from distraction by distraction.'[17] To quote from one response to
Princess Diana's death:

> It misses the point to say that she manipulated the media or sometimes
> sought media attention. She was used by the media, and more to the
> point, by the readers and viewers and listeners, by us, to provide sur-
> rogate intimacy, a substitute emotional life to fill up the emptiness of
> our own lives.
>
> The public was emotionally addicted to feeding off her—they
> exploited her. It was not the media, but the intimacy-starved emotional
> addicts who created the media demand for public intrusion into her
> life, who killed Diana.[18]

So, mirroring the first series of loss of differentiation between public and private in media professionals or their soul-bytes, there may be a corresponding
minestrone effect in the public. Again, permit me to articulate it in terms of
at least one dimension of some of the public's response to Princess Diana's
death:

Stage 1:   Public's acceptance of Diana's 2nd self
Stage 2:   Increasing involvement with Diana's 2nd self
Stage 3:   Addiction to Diana's 2nd self
Stage 4:   Mass-hysteric identification with Diana's 2nd self.

This doesn't matter all that much in situations like media hyping of characters from the sports, fashion or entertainment worlds, with mass-adulation on
the part of millions if not billions. Still, the danger of pragmatic communication slipping over into something much less morally neutral seems high. A
culture in which no critical questions are asked, in which there's dispropor-
tionate emphasis on the peripheral aspects of existence served by pragmatic
communication, can lead to the essential trivialization of public life, which is
our next topic.[19]

---

16 Ibid., p. 348.   17 *Collected Poems, 1909-1962* (London: Faber), 1974, p. 192.   18 Joe McCarroll,
'The Princess and the Saint,' *Irish Family*, 12 September1997.   19 An implication of both Andy Pollak's

INTOXICANT COMMUNICATION

As we know, what's often referred to as the fourth estate, the institution of a free and uncensored press, arose as a corrective to an older establishment of power. But the fourth estate is no freer from the desire to say *l'état c'est moi* than Louis XIV ever was.[20]

So as well as substantive communication, there can be disintegrative communication. What's going on here expresses a systematic underestimation if not downright contempt for its audience by some media professionals. But that underestimation, as we've suggested, may be colluded in by an audience that doesn't want to be addressed up to the full level of its humanity. The result of such collusion is a pseudo-community grounded in the lie. Let's have a look first at attempts at manipulation, by advertisers and politicians who themselves wish to instrumentalize the media.[21]

In his textbook on advertising, Ernest Dichter advises on how to flatter the customer:

> One of the strongest elements of a doctor's self-image is his perception of himself as a rational scientist ... He is particularly resentful, therefore, whenever a pharmaceutical house makes and disguises the emotional appeal to him. He is being treated no differently from the layman. He's being considered a gullible consumer ... In any communication with the doctor, pharmaceutical houses should therefore conceal emotional appeals beneath a cloak of rationality.[22]

And in the conversations with John Erlichman which President Nixon so thoughtfully recorded for posterity we get a fascinating glimpse of the ordinariness of attempted media management:

> P: I was talking to Bob—and Bob made the point ... In a sense it will be the evening news basically ... You know—you see a man looking honest and earnest, etc., denying it in a public forum.[23]

(cf. pp. 33-46) and Professor Schönbach's (cf. pp. 47-58) papers was that there is collusion between inciting media and incited audience in preferring passionate intemperance to rational reflection and just action. **20** Chapter 5 of Weaver's *News and the Culture of Lying*, is called 'Editocracy'. But the chastening account of President Kennedy's 'coldly mercenary relationship' towards the sycophantic *Newsweek* and later *Washington Post* editor, Benjamin Bradlee, indicates, perhaps, where the power really lies. (pp. 129-33). **21** As opposed to our earlier 'happy circle' of genuine communication 'from above', we can speak of a manipulative communication from above in terms of i) stupefying; ii) being stupefied; and iii) community of the lie. Weaver notes that 'The central fact about the interaction between news media and the people they cover is that *the people being covered know the media are watching and behave accordingly...*For their part *the news media are aware that newsmakers are performing, but they nonetheless treat newmakers' fabrications as authentic actions.*' (*News and the Culture of Lying*, [Weaver's italics] p. 6) **22** Ernest Dichter, *Handbook of Consumer Motivations* (New York: McGraw-Hill, 1964), p. 211. **23** *The White House Transcripts*, ed. Gerald Gold (New York: Bantam Books, 1974), p. 419.

E: We are at kind of an ebb tide right now in this whole thing, in terms of the media, as I see it. They are all a little afraid to get too far out on a limb on this ...and there's no new news breaking, and so they are kind of—
P: Waiting ...
E: Well sure, but now is a good time for us to fill that vacuum.
P: Oh, yes—a little news.[24]

We must maintain the integrity of the White House, and that integrity must be real, not transparent. There can be no whitewash at the White House.[25]

Advertisers and politicians, as President Nixon found out to his cost, aren't always successful, thanks to the alertness of the very media they attempt to manipulate, and of the audience they show such contempt for.

Remembering the Grand Inquisitor's comment in *The Brothers Karamazov* that nothing has ever been so burdensome as freedom, a freedom we can never jettison quickly enough, that media domination is often possible only with mass collusion from their audience. BBC *Newsnight*, years ago, carried a report on Lyndon Johnson's 1963 election campaign. This included a very effective TV commercial which showed a Russian girl picking flowers in a field, with a nuclear mushroom cloud suddenly appearing in the background. The clear implication was that if Barry Goldwater was elected, he'd nuke the USSR. The man who'd crafted this rhetorical flourish was asked if he didn't think he was manipulating people. 'Manipulation?', he replied, 'No. *Partip*ulation. The people *wanted* to be manipulated.'

What happens when the audience *is* taken in, *does* partipulate in the manipulation? Then there occurs an intensification of the original vicious circle of stupefying, being stupefied and community disintegration, now initiated by the public, dumbed-down to the dehumanized level they've been addressed to by their media.[26]

In Plato's dialogue, the *Apology*, Socrates is being tried by a court of 500 citizens on trumped up charges of atheism and corruption of the youth. What's interesting for us is Socrates' awareness that it's much harder to defend himself against the media-generated perception of him than against the particular charges. Aristophanes, a comic playwright, had created in *The Clouds* an

<hr/>

24 Ibid., p. 445.   **25** Ibid., p. 803.   **26** The corresponding vicious circle of manipulation 'from below', can be not only the desire to be manipulated, but also the dumbing-down effect of this on the media themselves. Then that manipulation 'from below' can itself take the dominant role of dumbing-down the media. Both media and audience can thus be caught in a mutual vicious circle or double-bind of i) stupefying; ii) being stupefied; and iii) community of the lie.

image of Socrates as just another idiotic and unprincipled intellectual on the make.[27]

Without direct contact with his life and works, the Athenian public was subjected to 25 years of attacks on Socrates. As a matter of fact, he'd spent his life opposing the kind of irresponsible intellectual he was portrayed as. But they voted for his execution. And it is this vicarious participation in the more or less deliberate lies of others that marks out the shared ethical disorder of media and their audience. That disorder colluded in by an undemanding audience achieves an amplified viciousness when certain sectors of the public give it concrete expression.[28]

Plato has diagnosed what's happening here as well as anyone. In the *Republic* (362a), he takes the situation where the most unjust man can hire the best media experts to present him as the most just person, at the same time defaming the most just person as the most unjust. While the just man wants not to seem, but to be, just, the unjust man wants to seem, not be, just. It's Plato's commentary on what happened to Socrates, since in Athens he was presented as worthy of death, while those who had been involved in politically motivated murders could present themselves as his just judges. Voegelin comments:

> The accent of reality has shifted so far from truth to the socially over-powering appearance—the dream tends to become reality … '[T]ruth,' in the sense of conformity of a man with himself, is achieved by the will to be unjust in order to harmonize with society … [T]o live in truth against appearance when the power of society is thrown on the side of appearance is a burden on the soul that is impossible to bear for the many, and hard to bear for the few. The pressure for conformity penetrates the soul and compels it to endow the *doxa* [appearance] experientially with *aletheia* [truth].[29]

On a lovely Sunday evening, in Nuremberg last September, I stood at the podium where Hitler had addressed his huge rallies in the '30s. It was the place to reflect on communication as intoxicant—a kind of contagion of the spiritual immune system in which the radical disorder of one individual is echoed by and evokes in others an equivalent inner darkness. Albert Speer, who organized these rallies, and stage-

---

27 A classic study of media-lynching is, of course, Heinrich Böll's *Die verlorene Ehre der Katharina Blum* (Munich: DTV, 1986). In the light of Professor Schönbach's examples (pp. 47-58), Böll's ironic opening disclaimer is as relevant as ever: 'The characters and events in this story are fictional. If the description of certain journalistic practices are similar to those of *Bild* newspaper, these similarities are neither intended nor accidental, but unavoidable' (Ibid., p. 5). 28 Professor Schönbach's statistics (cf. p. 48) on the rise of attacks on immigrant workers following media coverage of earlier attacks amply illustrates this effect. 29 Eric Voegelin, *Plato and Aristotle* (Baton Rouge: Louisiana State University Press, 1957), p. 79.

managed their presentation, has left a few remarks that, despite his own self-serving agenda, ring true. Speaking of Hitler, he writes:

> He gave the impression of a man whose whole purpose had been destroyed, who was continuing along his established orbit only because of the kinetic energy stored within him. Actually he had let go of the controls ... There was something actually insubstantial about him. But this was perhaps a permanent quality he had. In retrospect, I sometimes ask myself whether this intangibility, this insubstantiality, had not characterized him from early youth up to the moment of his suicide. He simply could not let anyone approach his inner being because that core was lifeless, empty.[30]

Speer recalls Leni Riefenstahl's studio filming of some of the principal speakers at the 1935 Party Congress later on, due to technical failures during the actual rally. He remarks of Rudolf Hess's performance:

> With his special brand of ardor, he turned precisely to the spot where Hitler would have been sitting, snapped to attention and cried: 'My Leader, I welcome you in the name of the Party Congress! ...' He did it all so convincingly that from that point on I was no longer sure of the genuineness of his feelings. The three others [Streicher, Rosenberg and Frank] also gave excellent performances in the emptiness of the studio, proving themselves gifted actors.[31]

So the individual hatewaves of the hollow men in control of communication were radiated to the public. What kind of a public? Søren Kierkegaard in nineteenth-century Copenhagen brilliantly diagnosed the anti-community of the lie constituted by the kind of manipulative/partipulative intoxicant communication indulged in by the National Socialist regime:

> In order that everything should be reduced to the same level, it is first of all necessary to procure a phantom, its spirit, a monstrous abstraction, an all-embracing something which is nothing, a mirage—and that phantom is *the public*. It is only in an age which is without passion, yet reflective, that such a phantom can develop itself with the help of the Press which itself becomes an abstraction ... Only when the sense of association in society is no longer strong enough to give life to concrete realities is the Press able to create that abstraction 'the public,' consisting of unreal individuals ... A public is everything and nothing,

---

30 Albert Speer, *Inside the Third Reich* (London: Sphere Books, 1979), p. 629.   31 Ibid., p. 105.

the most dangerous of all powers and the most insignificant: one can speak to a whole nation in the name of the public, and still the public will be less than a single real man, however unimportant...More and more individuals, owing to their bloodless indolence, will aspire to being nothing at all—in order to become the public ... The public is unrepentant, for it is not they who own the dog—they only subscribe. They neither set the dog on any one, nor whistle it off—directly ... And if the dog had to be killed they would say: it was really a good thing that bad-tempered dog was put down, everyone wanted it killed—even the subscribers.[32]

Of course we couldn't have such a 'public' here? Karl Kraus compared the service of the leading Viennese paper, so perfectly in harmony with the spiritual atrophy of the day, to that of a 'young, powerful, sympathetic masseuse.'[33] There's the virtual homogenization of the Irish weekday print media and of RTE's psych-jockeys[34] and commentators at a level of human flatness comparable to that of the *Neue Freie Presse*.[35] The cheerful harmony within this wasteland of cliché is a reminder that the *Neue Freie Presse* created, served and was deserved by its spiritually concussed audience.

RESTORING GENUINE CONVERSATION

However impermeable the anti-world of the lie generated by disintegrative media can seem, it's always possible to recover true public conversation again.[36] Socrates died, but the dialogue as a lived form of open democratic discussion survives. Ignazio Silone, Karl Kraus, the East European samizdat writers, all show that even under Fascist, National Socialist or Communist repression, it's still possible to maintain and restore substantive communication. And writers like Albert Camus in French, G.K. Chesterton and George Orwell in English, Pier Paolo Pasolini in Italian, contributed as much as anyone to keep-

---

32 *The Present Age* (New York: Harper Torchbooks, 1962), pp. 59-66.   33 *Die Fackel*, 36, March 1900, p. 15 (reprinted in *Die Fackel*, vol. 2, Kösel Verlag, Munich, 1968).   34 A phrase used by Walker Percy. His 'Last Donahue Show' in *Lost in the Cosmos* (New York: Washington Square Press, 1984, pp. 48-59) is hilariously relevant for the Irish 'public.'   35 Some would find the differences between say, RTE and the *Irish Independent*, or between the *Irish Times* and Independent Newspapers in general, more a matter of style than substance. Too many opinion-formers working in Irish media exhibit a rather uniform cultural orientation roughly characterizable as eighteenth-century anti-religious, nineteenth-century progressivist-scientistic, twentieth-century ostensive compassion. It's a mixture a reasonably large slice of the Irish public is comfortable with. 36 Recalling Michael Oakeshott's understanding of civilization as a conversation, where the relations 'are not those of assertion and denial, but the conversational relationships of acknowledgment and accommodation' (*Rationalism in Politics*, Indianapolis: Liberty Press, 1991, p. 187).

ing open critique alive in their societies. Encouraged by their work, maybe it might be possible to formulate a *Code of Conduct for the Well-Tempered Journalist*:

- Being a journalist doesn't excuse me from being a person-in-dialogue.
- Belonging to the audience for media communications doesn't excuse me from being a person-in-dialogue either.
- Don't economize with the truth to others as you wouldn't want them to economize with the truth to you.
- A Brno journalist, Blanka Pinosova, supplied me with a fourth point, from a Czech writer, Jan Werich: 'It's not possible to overcome stupidity, but neither can we stop trying to struggle against it, otherwise stupidity will invade the whole world.'
- Learn off by heart the words of the prophet Ezekiel (33:7-9): 'So you, son of man, I have made a watchman for the house of Israel; whenever you hear a word from my mouth, you shall give them warning from me. If I say to the wicked, O wicked man, you shall surely die, and you do not speak to warn the wicked to turn from his way, that wicked man shall die in his iniquity, but his blood I will require at your hand. But if you warn the wicked to turn from his way, and he does not turn from his way, he shall die in his iniquity, but you will have saved your soul.'

An invitation to racism? Irish daily newspaper coverage of the refugee issue

ANDY POLLAK

I should begin by declaring an interest: the subject of refugees is one I do not approach with the cold eye of the professional journalist. In 1948, my father, himself a former Communist who had been badly wounded in the Spanish Civil War and whose Jewish family had been scattered by the Second World War, had to flee his native land—Czechoslovakia—because its Communist government and police did not like the things he was writing in his Prague newspaper. He was let into the United Kingdom after the lucky intervention of an English peer stopped the immigration authorities sending him back on the next plane to Prague, and so began a new life with my mother in Northern Ireland. For the next ten years he was a 'stateless' person travelling on a Geneva Convention travel document.

So I am a kind of insider/outsider. Passionately proud of my Irishness, yet with the kind of background which allows me to some extent, at least, to empathise with the plight of refugees. I hope that does not prevent me from critically examining the Irish press coverage of the refugee issue with fairness and respect for the facts.

I think the record shows that the independent state of Ireland had until the last few years a poor—and occasionally shameful—record of keeping its doors firmly closed to all but a tiny trickle of people fleeing persecution and terror. Anyone who saw Louis Lentin's recent RTE film about successive Irish governments' refusal to take in Jewish refugees in the thirties, forties and fifties will know what I mean.

There is an attitude in Ireland which survives from those days. It is a cosy, often xenophobic, 'Ireland for the Irish' kind of attitude. One highly educated refugee from the former Yugoslavia, an anthropologist, touched on it recently when he called us 'an insular people, ignorant when it comes to dealing with and living with other cultures'. The most famous example of it was Mr Deasy in *Ulysses* telling Stephen Daedalus that Ireland never had a Jewish problem because 'we never let them in'. More recent examples range from the Department of Justice's chilling refusal to allow 100 orphaned children, survivors of Belsen, a temporary refuge in Ireland in the late 1940s—calling Jews 'a potential irritant in the body politic'—to the language and attitudes of Áine

33

Ní Chonaill, the teacher from West Cork who wants to keep all but a very few immigrants and refugees out of Ireland.

Such an attitude co-exists with a smug feeling that because Irish people give a lot of money to Third World aid agencies and have a history of anti-colonial struggle, we are somehow more righteous on issues like race and refugees than the nasty Brits and other European nations with an imperialist past.

However, this little island, despite its much vaunted enthusiasm for all things European and its supposed empathy with the post-colonial countries of the developing world, still contains many people who feel deeply uncomfortable with the prospect of Ireland entering the European multi-cultural mainstream, with all its richness, diversity and daunting problems of race, class and community fragmentation.

My thesis in this address is that some of these people are in powerful positions in the Irish media, and particularly in the country's largest and most influential newspaper group, Independent Newspapers. I hope to show that the treatment of the refugee issue, particularly by newspapers in that group, did a considerable amount to change the benign, if ignorant, attitude of most Irish people to refugees into something much more volatile and potentially dangerous in the short space of less than 12 months.

Until late 1996 the arrival of refugees in Ireland was a non-story. For the most part, the great Irish public knew and cared little about the tiny groups of government-sponsored refugees who arrived here from Hungary in the 1950s, Chile in the 1970s and Vietnam and Iran in the 1980s.

In the 'new Ireland' of the 1990s, the overwhelming consensus was that people found racism both abhorrent and alien to the Irish world view. Father Micheál Mac Gréil, the Jesuit sociologist and author of the seminal 1977 work *Prejudice and Tolerance in Ireland*, found in his 1996 update of that study that there had been 'a significant and substantial decrease in racialism' in the intervening twenty years. He suggested that this was partly due to positive black role models like Nelson Mandela, soccer player Paul McGrath and rock musician Phil Lynott.

In the reporting of the first racially-motivated attacks in the mid-nineties, it was made very clear where reporters' sympathies lay. Thus in April 1995 a report in the *Irish Independent* about a Jamaican couple being driven out of their Dublin city flat and the resulting protests began: 'This is the fight against fascism in Dublin in 1995.'

The following month a *Sunday Independent* feature on the growing levels of racism in Dublin quoted the revulsion of residents of the building where the Jamaicans had been living; the condemnations of local councillors; the opinions of an official of the Council for Overseas Students; and the conclusions of Father Mac Gréil.

Until very recently there was also no refugee problem in Ireland: they were 'out of sight, out of mind'. I may be wrong, but I think I wrote the first detailed article, back in September 1996, about the relatively recent influx of hundreds of refugees from countries like Cuba, Somalia, Algeria, the Congo, Romania and the former Soviet Union. Ireland's sudden image as an attractive place of refuge was due to a number of factors: neighbouring countries like Britain and France tightening their asylum laws, our new reputation as Europe's 'tiger' economy, the glowing international image of President Mary Robinson, even the widely-reported political and sporting breakthroughs of the IRA cease-fire and the World Cup performances of the Irish soccer team.

The sharp rise, from an extremely low base, of the number of people seeking asylum in Ireland is now well-known : from 39 in 1992, to 91 in 1993, to 355 in 1994, to 424 in 1995, to 1,179 in 1996, to 3,883 in 1997.

However, it was not until the spring of 1997 that the refugee story really began to take off in Ireland's national newspapers. That April stories began to appear regularly about the alarmingly rapid increase in the number of asylum-seekers. Joan Burton, the then junior minister at the Department of Justice—and an outspoken champion of fairer and more generous asylum procedures—admitted she was 'very worried' that organized groups were targeting Ireland as an easy country to smuggle people into. The Department was asking the Gardaí to increase surveillance at Irish ports in order to stem the greatly increased inflow.

However, the *Irish Times* warned of the need to keep a sense of proportion about this 'supposed immigration problem'. In an editorial on 18 April, the paper wrote:

> The State is not about to be overrun by a tidal wave of foreigners who will undermine the daily fabric of our lives. Compared to any of our EU partners, we are dealing with scarcely more than a trickle of immi-gration. Ireland still has fewer—far fewer—asylum seekers than most other European countries. If nothing else, the current phenomenon only serves to underline how we have conspicuously failed to take our fair share of refugees and asylum seekers in the past.

This appeal for a sense of proportion would fall on deaf ears in the months ahead. This seems to have been due to two factors: firstly, the whipping up of the refugee issue in the election campaign which began in mid-May by a small number of unscrupulous politicians in the Dublin area; and secondly, the dis-covery of the refugee story by the country's largest newspaper group: Independent Newspapers, largely owned by Tony O'Reilly. Independent Newspapers controls the largest circulation daily, the *Irish Independent*; the only Dublin evening paper, the *Evening Herald*, the two largest circulation

Sunday papers, the *Sunday Independent* and the *Sunday World* , and has a major shareholding in the only national tabloid, the *Star*. The Independent Group accounts for no less than two-thirds of the national daily newspapers sold in this state and—when its minority share in the *Sunday Tribune* is included—a massive 95 per cent of the Irish-owned Sunday newspaper market.

One of the *Irish Independent's* first substantial offerings came on 5 May under the title 'Gardaí move on dole fraud day trip "refugees".' Gardaí and government officials were quoted as investigating 'foreign criminals posing as refugees and claiming welfare benefits'. The story said at least two dozen Nigerians and Algerians were travelling from Britain, sometimes daily, to fraudulently claim thousands of pounds every week.

From the outset the paper's emphasis was on an alleged link between bogus 'refugees'—the word was usually placed between inverted commas—criminals and welfare fraud. This story set the tone for the paper's future coverage of the refugee issue in three other ways: it was written, as would most of the news reports on the issue, by the paper's security correspondent; it uncritically quoted Garda or government—usually Department of Justice—sources; and it emphasised that the main reason for refugees coming to Ireland was to take advantage of our supposedly 'generous' welfare payment system. (I don't know if it is generous or not—I haven't seen the systems of other countries compared in any article).

Ironically, an editorial on the same day was remarkably liberal, condemning 'immigrants' who defrauded the welfare system, but also prophesying that one day an Irish writer or artist with a Bosnian or Romanian name might bring the country as much credit as a Joyce or a Yeats.

The *Irish Independent's* next major report, five days later, was entitled 'Inmates lobby to stay in jail as refugees fill up hostels.' Despite the heading, the lead paragraph made no mention of refugees—it was about serious overcrowding in Mountjoy's female prison. However, the second paragraph went on: 'Efforts to relieve the overcrowding through temporary release have merely resulted in some women prisoners lobbying to stay in jail because foreign asylum-seekers are being given preference on hostel places—leaving nowhere for prisoners to go when they are freed.' There was not a single quote, nor a single source cited, to back up this claim, although it seems to have emerged from the annual conference of the Prison Officers' Association. The result was that prison overcrowding and pressure on homeless accommodation were added to crime and welfare fraud on the list of refugees' sins in the *Irish Independent* reader's mind.

Nobody is denying that there was a real problem caused by the sudden, large influx of refugees, which was crying out to be reported. On 14 May, the *Irish Times* reported that there had been what the IMPACT trade union called a 'near riot' when an Eastern Health Board office in Dublin providing welfare payments to refugees had to close because it could not deal with the numbers queuing up outside.

But there is reporting and reporting. The following day Paddy O'Gorman, who presents the excellent 'Queuing for a Living' on RTE radio, wrote a carefully balanced piece in the *Examiner* pointing out how unwise it was for the health board to make refugees queue for their money beside homeless Irish people; noting the problem the Gardaí faced with some smart and apparently well-educated Romanian gypsies; and telling the story of a young Somali man who had spent six weeks in a container at a cost of 2,000 dollars to get to Ireland.

May 23rd saw the beginning of the first of two weekends of real hysteria over the refugee influx in Irish newspapers. By this time there was a general election in full sway, so there should have been plenty of 'bread and butter' issues to hold the media's attention. Perhaps it was rather a boring campaign and the newspapers were looking round for something a little juicier. They were helped by a number of unscrupulous Fianna Fáil and Progressive Democrat candidates looking for easy, populist votes by talking up the refugee problem.

Whatever it was, the security correspondent of the *Irish Independent* led off the weekend coverage with a piece quoting 'growing fears' by immigration officials (i.e. the Department of Justice) that 'the country is on the brink of a major refugee problem.' For the third time since February, he used the same phrase—'Gardaí are increasingly worried at the growing involvement of refugees in street crime and prostitution'. There was not a single direct quote from a senior Garda officer or a single example of a conviction against a refugee to back up this very strong allegation.

The following day the *Irish Independent*'s 'Weekender' supplement weighed in with a 'special report' on the 'refugee crisis'. It started off with an encounter with a 'new, determined style of beggar', an eight-year-old Romanian girl in this case, as if a Romanian child begging in the streets was a typical refugee. If the numbers coming in were to continue at the present rate, the writer declared, 'hundreds of thousands of refugees would be here by the end of the decade'.

The *Sunday World*, another O'Reilly-owned paper, weighed in the following day with a page one headline '5,000 refugees flooding to Ireland'. 'Many are paying out big money for false passports provided by ruthless gangs of criminals in mainland Europe', it continued. 'The immigrant flood is costing Ireland millions, with the state forking out up to £100 a night to provide some refugees with hotel beds'. A double-page spread inside opened under the subheading 'Floodgates open as a new army of poor swamp the country'.

On the Monday morning, my own paper—usually so careful and sober—appeared to succumb to the prevailing mood. A full page of articles carried headlines reading 'Influx of asylum-seekers causes concern'; 'Dublin now main target for gangs trafficking in people'; and 'Shopkeepers say theft by Romanians is snowballing'. Rather than leaving coverage of the issue to its specialist, Paul Cullen—who would later win a European Year against Racism prize for his coverage of the issue—the *Irish Times* brought in other reporters who had to rely on Department of Justice and Garda sources. 'The word is out. Ireland is the place to come', said one Garda source, the apparent basis for the use of the word 'main' in the headline. However, the same report also noted that 'the level of smuggling of people into the Republic is considered low'.

This momentary lapse by the *Irish Times* seems to have been caused by a situation which every daily newspaper journalist knows. He or she comes in for a Sunday shift—when news is often thin on the ground—and is instructed by a panicky news editor who has seen the weekend's blanket coverage of a particular issue, to go out and do better. Again I must stress that I am not saying the major issue of the increased number of refugees should not have been reported—all I am saying is that it should have been done with sensitivity, care and balance. I will come in a minute to one huge gap which led to a lack of balanced reporting.

Within a few days, that splendid columnist, Fintan O'Toole, was doing his bit to restore some balance with a piece about the 'breathtaking hypocrisy' of the Irish. He pointed out that 3,000 new arrivals in two and a half years was hardly 'swamping' a population of three and a half million. He noted that eight short years earlier, when we had net emigration of 44,000, 'we went through paroxysms of national outrage at the plight of illegal economic migrants in America. We button-holed every senator and congressman with an eye on the Irish vote and expressed our sense of betrayal at America's refusal to accept as many of our economic refugees as we chose to send her'.

He also wondered at the 'rather sickening sight of people who never gave a twopenny damn for the homeless and the poor suddenly discovering them. The cry goes up that this influx of economic migrants is taking resources that rightly belong to our very own poor people.'

The *Irish Independent* was not fazed. 'Taxpayers to face bills of £20m-plus for refugee flood', declared a banner headline on 31 May. This was Joan Burton's estimate, although the reporter quoted health and social welfare officials saying it could be more than £50 million.

And what about this for a paragraph full of unconvincing sources, unsourced claims and menacing innuendoes? 'Sources at the forefront of the battle to cope with the influx of refugees said they were being overwhelmed by the sheer weight of numbers, many of them apparent bogus asylum seekers, and warned that the genuine refugees, who account for only one in ten by international standards, were facing the danger of a backlash because of the wave of immigrants.'

The following weekend, despite the fact that the papers were full of the previous day's election count and analysis, was another new low for Irish journalism in its coverage of the refugee issue. This time the *Irish Times* stood apart, with two excellent pieces by Paul Cullen featuring interviews with refugees and pleas from them to politicians to stop using their plight as an election issue. The Serbo-Croat anthropologist I mentioned earlier, who had suffered the trauma of being used as a human shield between the Yugoslav army and the Croats, was quoted as telling Department of Justice officials who were accusing him of being an economic refugee: 'I had a flat, a family and a good job in Yugoslavia. Why would I give that all up for some social welfare here?'

Over in the *Evening Herald* they were re-running the previous week's *Irish Independent* story, complete with banner headlines, about refugees getting £20 million in welfare pay-outs.

The following day's front page headline in the *Irish Independent* screamed: 'Crackdown on 2,000 "sponger" refugees.' 'The Department of Justice clampdown comes amid fears of a huge influx of immigrants attracted here by the country's generous welfare payments,' the article declared. In fact just one Romanian refugee had been deported. The only basis for the figure in the headline was the ubiquitous security officials estimating that 'in the longer term ... between two and three thousand refugees will be turned down for asylum and sent back to their home countries.' Can you imagine the terror such a headline would have induced among the country's 3-4,000 asylum seekers, with its dreadful forecast that the vast majority of them would eventually be sent back to the countries from which they had fled?

The next day's *Sunday Independent* tried in its hamfisted way to see things from the refugee's viewpoint. This did not mean some careful, in-depth interviews with the refugees themselves. It involved a young woman reporter dressing up as a Romanian refugee and begging in Dublin's streets. If a British newspaper had dressed up a reporter as a down-and-out 'Paddy' and gone out panhandling on the streets of London, can you imagine the outcry from the politically correct in Britain and the Irish everywhere?

The hysterical headlines continued for a month or so after the election. The worst offenders continued to be the Independent Group: 'Refugee flood to spark homes crisis, report warns' proclaimed one *Irish Independent* front page headline. 'Refugees "flooding" maternity hospitals', screamed the *Evening Herald*.

Inevitably the tabloids joined in. Probably the single most absurd, extreme, fear-inducing headline of the year came in the *Star* on 13 June. Under the headline 'Refugee Rapists on the Rampage', it quoted 'top Garda sources' as saying prostitutes and minors were the main target of 'rapacious Romanians and Somalians' and warning Dublin women to 'stay away from refugees after a spree of sex assaults'. The article mentioned no charges, no convictions, and on closer scrutiny the top Garda sources turned out to be one Garda in Fitzgibbon Street Station. The same report appeared in the *Irish Independent* on the same day, again based on the comments of one unnamed Garda in the same station.

It was little wonder then that towards the end of June, the Irish Committee for the European Year against Racism felt it necessary to call a press conference to express their dismay at recent newspaper coverage of the refugee issue. The Irish co-ordinator, Philip Watt, said some of the coverage 'can at best be described as irresponsible and at worst outright racist in content'. Other reports had been balanced and well-researched, 'only to be undermined by the application of an alarmist or sensationalized headline or sub-heading'. The *Irish Independent*, of course, did not carry a line on the press conference.

The change in atmosphere during the first half of 1997—noted by all the refugees I have talked to, even the longest resident and most contented and pro-Irish of them—was summed up by one Congolese who said the friendly welcome he had received when he had arrived in Dublin three years previously made it seem as though he was 'walking in my home town'. But now he was frequently addressed as 'nigger', accused of stealing jobs from Irish people and four months earlier had been beaten up by two men. He blamed the media for 'creating tensions'. A mother of a mixed-race son accused the media of being 'like racist cheerleaders' and was particularly critical of newspaper headlines and phone-in programmes like the *Pat Kenny Show* on RTE and the *Chris Barry Show* on FM 104.

The second half of 1997 saw a more measured journalistic response to the refugee issue. This was partly due to its becoming less of a headline-making story as successive Ministers for Justice, Nora Owen and John O'Donoghue, increased surveillance at ports and borders in order to clamp down on new refugee arrivals. This did not prevent the *Sunday Independent*, in a piece on 3 September headed 'Garda purge on bogus refugees' and full of references to illegal 'aliens', estimating wildly that the number of asylum seekers expected in Ireland by the end of the year had now risen to 7,500 (in the event the official number turned out to be just over half that figure, 3,883).

In the same week the *Examiner* quoted a taxi driver involved in smuggling refugees from the North. He told the reporter: 'We have been smuggling cattle for 30 years—why should a black man be any harder'. The previous May in a piece about problems with Romanian thieves and beggars, the *Irish Times* had quoted a Dublin street trader saying: 'If you look in their heads, from the youngest up, you'll see £500 or £600 worth of teeth, all in gold'. I'm not for a moment suggesting that such appalling comments should not be reported— all I'm saying is that somewhere in our newspapers—and I haven't seen it yet— some editorialist or commentator should point out that it was just such attitudes which created the atmosphere leading to the euthanasia programmes and death camps in Germany and Austria in the thirties and forties.

As President Mary McAleese said in February 1998, the sight of Irish people, so long used to being demonized and hurtfully labelled themselves, doing the same to refugees and travellers, was 'particularly, tragically unedifying'. Only the *Irish Times* carried her speech. Two months earlier her equally strong comments at the closing ceremony of the European Year against Racism about her family's own experience as refugees from the violence of Belfast at the beginning of the Northern 'troubles' had also been ignored by the Independent group.

I have nearly come to the end of this embarrassing litany of sloppy, sensationalist and sometimes mischief-making reporting and sub-editing. There are a couple of final classic examples. On 29 November, the *Irish Independent* carried a full-page feature in its Weekender supplement entitled 'The Refugee Smugglers'. This unsavoury and ill-researched piece was guaranteed to touch every ill-informed reader's most fearful panic button. Under sinister-looking pictures of a deserted Amiens Street at night—'Refugee Alley', the caption called it—and cowled, djellaba-wearing figures, it claimed that 50 people per week, and up to 200 people in some weeks, were being smuggled into Dublin's north inner-city in 'a well-organized scam ... They arrive at night in cars and vans with Northern registration numbers'.

The absurdity of this claim is immediately apparent. At this rate over 2,500 and maybe up to five, six, or seven thousand people would have arrived in north inner-city Dublin alone during 1997. Compare this to the actual total 1997 figure of under 3,900 asylum seekers for the country as a whole.

'There are heavy people involved in this business, both here and in the North. They are the same people who have been involved in drugs and other criminal activity and this is a new outlet for them,' one local councillor was quoted as saying. A local businessman was 'not willing to be named for fear of reprisals'. Here are all the classic ingredients for stirring up a bout of xenophobia in a poor working-class area: large numbers of strange foreigners and bogus refugees being smuggled in by violent, drug-dealing criminals and dangerous people from Northern Ireland.

The final touch was added by a north Dublin TD, Ivor Callely, who earlier that week had called for 'rogue' asylum-seekers, who were 'carrying on in a culture that is not akin to Irish culture' (he instanced begging and 'bleeding of lambs in the back garden', although he had received no direct reports of the latter practice) to be 'kicked out' of Ireland.

In his contribution to the *Irish Independent* article, Mr Callely was allowed to get away with the inflammatory statement: 'There is such resentment about this in the inner city that I'm concerned that there will be a serious outbreak of violence of some kind'.

The TD made one final unsubstantiated claim: Ireland, he said, has 'a higher proportion of asylum seekers than most European countries.' The facts, which the *Irish Independent* failed to ascertain, are otherwise. In 1996, Ireland came fifth from bottom among the 15 EU countries when it came to total numbers of asylum applications, with only Finland, Italy, Portugal and tiny Luxembourg behind us. We had 1,179 applications, compared to over 149,000 in Germany, nearly 35,000 in the UK, 22,000 in the Netherlands, 17,400 in France, 12,400 in Belgium, and 5,893 in Denmark, a country of comparable wealth and population, which thus had more than five times more applications than Ireland.

In 1997—the year in which Irish newspaper columns were full of wild claims that Ireland was being 'flooded' and 'swamped' with refugees—according to preliminary figures from the United Nations High Commission for Refugees, Ireland stayed at exactly the same position in the European table: our 3,883 asylum applications compared poorly to similar countries like Denmark which received 4,800, Austria which received 6,700, Belgium nearly 12,000 and the Netherlands 35,000. I have to say that in all my study of press coverage of the refugee issue in 1997 and early 1998, I did not once see such comparative European figures spelled out in detail. This surely was a major failure by the press to inform the public in a balanced way about the extent of the so-called refugee 'crisis' in this country.

After nine months of fear-inducing coverage of the refugee issue, it will have come as little surprise when the *Irish Independent's* 1997 end of year opinion poll found that a large majority of Irish people now had very negative attitudes towards refugees. Under a page one heading 'Most oppose "open door" policy on refugees', the poll showed that nearly two-thirds of those questioned felt it was reasonable to send refugees back to the EU country in which they had first arrived. This was the EU agreement, the appropriately named Dublin Convention, which would allow Ireland to rid itself of the bulk of its incoming refugees at a bureaucratic stroke. A tiny one in ten of those polled—11 per cent—believed that all or most asylum seekers are genuine in that they face danger or persecution in their native countries.

The article containing the poll findings also had a political message. In previous weeks there had been reports that Mary Harney, the Tánaiste or deputy Prime Minister, had been arguing in cabinet for an amnesty for all or most refugees already in Ireland on the grounds that since so many countries had taken Irish economic migrants, it was morally indefensible for Ireland to refuse to take refugees. The *Irish Independent* political correspondent warned that she was now 'aware from soundings around the country of strong voter resistance' to this. The mandarins in the Department of Justice, the fiercest opponents of such an amnesty, must have been delighted.

On 23 January 1998 Paul Cullen in the *Irish Times* spelled out one major, and so far largely unreported and unanalysed, reason for Ireland's refugee problem. He quoted from a new book by Trinity College Dublin (TCD) law lecturer Rosemary Byrne, an authority on discrimination and refugee law, in which she said that administrative paralysis in government, rather than the arrival of asylum-seekers, had created the refugee crisis. The 3,883 people who sought asylum in Ireland in 1997 was a 'staggering' increase in the Irish context, given that we were starting from such a very low base, she said, but it was 'comparatively light' compared to other EU countries. I have already detailed those very revealing comparative figures.

Ms Byrne wrote: 'As the Government fails to identify those most in need of protection within a reasonable time framework, so too it has allowed those with no valid claim under the Refugee Act to remain in the State, fuelling mis-informed intolerance towards the broader refugee community'.

Which brings us to the final element in the coverage of the refugee issue in the past year: the coverage of what I would see as the inevitable emergence of a xenophobic, semi-racist political group to campaign against refugees. This group, the Immigration Control Platform, is led by Áine Ní Chonaill, a West Cork schoolteacher, who appears to want the numbers of all resident foreigners to be severely restricted: she objects to English hippies and British and German nationals, as well as to refugees.

When her new group provocatively held its first public meeting in Ennis, the gateway to Ireland for many asylum-seekers through Shannon Airport, the press coverage was unsympathetic. The strong-arm antics of a group of young ultra-leftists who prevented her tiny group from meeting did more than anything to get her a hearing: notably on the country's most-watched television programme, the *Late Late Show*, where I am told—I did not see it myself— that Gay Byrne gave her a noticeably sympathetic reception.

'Face of Hate' was the *Star*'s huge front page headline, beside an unflattering picture of Ms Ní Chonaill, the day after the Ennis meeting—'Bigot who wants to kick refugees out'. Inside was a report which pointed out that Ms Ní Chonaill had won only a handful of votes when she ran in the 1997 General Election, and quoted people from the Irish Refugee Council, the Association of Refugees and Asylum Seekers, the Irish Centre for Migration Studies, the Rescue Trust and Amnesty International. The report was at fault only in that it did not give Ms Ní Chonaill any right of reply.

The paper's editorial was a model of fair-minded thinking. It pointed out that 'the Irish have more reason than any nation on earth to extend a welcome to immigrants—because there is not a country in the world which hasn't embraced our citizens with open arms.' Stressing that it did not favour an open door policy, it nevertheless urged 'a set of fair and proper rules' to allow Ireland to give a new life to unfortunate refugees. In this way 'we will repay the debt we owe to the rest of the world for its help in our many times of need.'

Unfortunately a few pages further on we were back to stereotypes and scaremongering. A double-page spread under the headline 'Borders collapse under refugee invasion' featured a map catchlined 'Fortress Europe leaking like a sieve.' This World War Two-style battle map was full of black 'flash-point' arrows to mark the points where armies of refugees were sweeping across Europe from Africa, the Middle East and Eastern Europe. There seemed to be little awareness, despite the thoughtful editorial, that such a pre-sentation could only feed the kind of paranoia which makes the arguments of the likes of Jean Marie Le Pen and Áine Ní Chonaill attractive to ignorant people.

Do not underestimate the power of the press. I heard the *Evening Herald's* claim that pregnant refugees were flooding Dublin's maternity hospitals repeated several times by callers to phone-in programmes during the 1997 presidential election. I was disappointed, for example, at the unwillingness of Dana, when she received one such call on Vincent Browne's RTE programme, to take the issue on and at the very least reproach the caller for his lack of Christian compassion.

I have also seen anti-refugee articles—for example an editorial from the Irish edition of an unidentified British tabloid in June 1997 headlined 'Slam the door on spongers'—used as crude racist leaflets which are pushed through letter-boxes in inner city Dublin. The editorial-cum-leaflet had scrawled across it: 'Do you want Dublin to become like London overrun with niggers. Then do something about it'. An anti-refugee group which picketed the Summerhill social security offices in central Dublin in the same month carried a banner reproducing a front page headline from the Irish edition of the *News of the World* which read 'Irish race riot fear'.

In contrast, I want to say one thing about my own paper's editorials during this period. I have already been critical of one day's *Irish Times* coverage in May 1997. I also agree with the views of a letter-writer on 12 May 1997 who criticised the paper for juxtaposing and interchanging the words 'illegal', 'immi-grant' and 'refugee' in a haphazard and unthought-out way. The law here is extremely complex. However the 1951 Refugee Convention asks governments not to penalize people who have to cross national frontiers illegally and break immigration laws in order to flee persecution. The Irish Refugee Council, and in practice the Irish Government, treats people as legal residents as soon as they apply for asylum and for as long as that application is being considered. The media should follow suit.

But at the risk of being accused of smugness and self-congratulation, I have to say that while researching this address I found the *Irish Times* editorials on it to be generally careful, even-handed and not afraid to castigate politicians, senior civil servants and even the media when that was needed.

Thus, as early as 6 June, the *Irish Times* leader-writer was criticising 'a number of intemperate outbursts from public representatives, who ought to be much more aware of how over-generalizing and stereotyping images of strangers can play a part in creating or encouraging racist attitudes.' It accused the Department of Justice of having run immigration policy for many years 'secretively and highly restrictively' in close conjunction with the British Government. And it urged lawmakers and leaders of public opinion to 'distinguish carefully between the great majority of law-abiding refugees and the small minority who break Irish law and must be subject to its rigours if they do so.'

One of the most influential leaders of public opinion in the Republic of Ireland is the Independent Newspapers Group, with its dominant position in the daily paper market and its near-monopoly stranglehold over the national Sunday paper market. To use TCD lawyer Rosemary Byrne's phrase, I think the evidence shows that the Independent Group, at the very least, 'fuelled misinformed intolerance' of refugees over the past year. There were far too many sensational headlines, misleading statistics, unsourced claims, and often plain demonizing of asylum-seekers. Refugees, a small, frightened and powerless group in Irish society had no comeback against the big guns of the country's most powerful media combine.

There are a couple of mitigating circumstances that should be mentioned. Everyone knows—although it is a knowledge not always shared outside our trade—that newspapers are produced under pressure, and editors and sub-editors working at night often have to make quick decisions about headlines or cutting a reporter's copy (although this should not excuse sensationalist front page headlines which are long pondered over). There has been more than one example of reporters being outraged at the way their articles on sensitive refugee issues have been headlined and butchered under pressure of time and space.

Secondly, the issues of refugees and racism are relatively new to Irish journalists. We have much to learn about the potentially dangerous nuances of language in this situation, about being aware that a careless phrase, a sensational headline, an insufficiently checked source can reinforce prejudice and ignite racial hate. My impression is that most of us were much more conscious of the sensitivities involved at the end of 1997 than we were at the beginning.

Having said that, I want to quote Seamus Dooley, the National Union of Journalists' national organizer in Ireland, and himself an *Irish Independent* journalist until the end of 1997. I share Dooley's concern that in covering the refugee issue too many Irish journalists have relied too much and too uncritically on official, often unnamed sources, usually in the Gardaí or the Department of Justice, and have failed to challenge ill-informed and often highly prejudiced statements from civil servants, politicians and policemen.

In a paper to an Amnesty International conference, Dooley looked more closely at the *Star*'s 'Refugee Rapists on the Rampage' story. He said the failure in that story—apart from the deeply offensive headline—was the uncrit-

46ical acceptance of the Fitzgibbon Street Station Garda's statement. Why was such a strong and extreme statement not challenged? Did the statement that women 'should be wary of anyone saying they were either Somalian or Romanian' represent official policy? What was the view of the Garda Commissioner or the Minister for Justice?

'Did the statement "They [the refugees] should be deported immediately rather than being let back on the streets where they will strike again" represent more than the extreme view of one unenlightened Garda?' asked Dooley. Did it merit the sub-head 'Gardaí warn women of new foreign threat'? And finally, and perhaps most importantly, why was no response sought from the refugee agencies or the refugees themselves?

The *Star* article was a particularly extreme example of dozens of reports on refugee-related issues carried by Irish newspapers, and particularly those belonging to Independent Newspapers, during 1997. The searching questions Seamus Dooley asks could be applied to any of those articles, and to the journalists who wrote them and the editors who commissioned and placed them in their papers.

I believe we are at a sensitive moment in an Irish society which is trying to come to terms with the difficult, rapid but exciting changes brought about by an unprecedented level of prosperity and a relatively new outward-looking involvement with a multicultural Europe. As one of the most outstanding spokesman of the refugee community in Ireland, Dr Mohammed Al-Sad'r, said in a recent interview—'It is only through nipping racism in the bud early, and through education, understanding, dialogue and admitting mistakes when they are made that Ireland can be a safe home for all its white, black, yellow, red, Protestant, Catholic, Jewish and Muslim people.'

In an editorial in September 1997, the *Irish Times* said something similar. It pointed out that the refugee debate is 'as much about us as the asylum-seekers who increasingly want to come here. What kind of Ireland do we want for the new millennium? Is it to be a multi-cultural society? If so, how is this inclusiveness to be achieved? Discussion of these issues has hardly begun.'

Not only has it not begun—I believe it has been put back by Independent Newspapers pandering to the most fearful and xenophobic strands in our island people's character. If anyone wants to do something small but practical to start to change that, I suggest he or she could do worse than write and complain to the group's proprietor, Tony O'Reilly, until recently head of the Heinz Corporation, and strong supporter, through his South African chain of newspapers, of Nelson Mandela and the struggle against apartheid.

Agenda-setting, agenda-reinforcing, agenda-deflating? Ethical dimensions of the media's role in public opinion

KLAUS SCHÖNBACH

During 1992-93 violence broke out in a number of German cities. Refugee housing areas in Hoyerswerda, Saxony and Rostock on the Baltic Sea were besieged and asylum-seekers had to flee from their burning homes. In two other German cities, Mölln and Solingen, houses inhabited by Turks were set on fire. Eleven people died. Immediately after the shocking events in Hoyerswerda, Rostock and Solingen, the number of criminal acts against foreigners in Germany did not—as one would expect—decrease. On the contrary, there was a dramatic rise (Figure 1).

How did those who decided to resort to violence against foreigners in one city know that the asylum-seekers had just been 'successfully' attacked in other German cities? In a country of 80 million people, it must be assumed that this information was conveyed by the media. But why did people feel not only *informed* about the events, but also *encouraged* to take action themselves against foreigners? Was this also due to the media? What was the media coverage of those incidents like, and more generally, how did the German media report on the refugee issue during 1992 and 1993? A good example of the problematic role of the media is provided by the *BILD-Zeitung*, the largest tabloid in Europe. It sells about 4.5 million copies a day, and about a quarter of Germans aged 14 years and older read it regularly. Typical *BILD* headlines in 1992 and 1993 (Figure 2) focused on three assumptions related to foreigners in Germany, headlines that were repeated over and over again:

- The first assumption was: 'there are too many asylum-seekers in Germany, and many more are flooding into the country'.
- The second depicted asylum seekers as at least ungrateful, even as cheats. The message was not very subtle: 'they are not political refugees but lazy people who want to avail of German social benefits'.
- The third described the native population as suffering and as a result: 'people have to leave their homes so that asylum-seekers can be housed'. In addition, the crime rate was said to be increasing.

Figure 1: Criminal acts against foreigners in Germany 1991-3

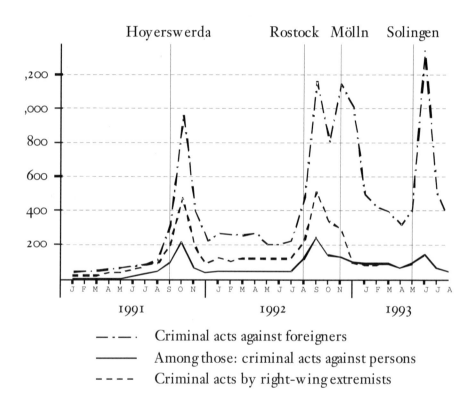

—·—· Criminal acts against foreigners

——— Among those: criminal acts against persons

---- Criminal acts by right-wing extremists

Source: Public opinion and violence against foreigners in re-unified Germany: empirical comments on an unclear relationship (*Bevölkerungsmeinung und Gewalt gegen Ausländer im wiedervereinigten Deutschland: Empirishe Anmerkungen zu einem unklaren Verhältnis*), T. Ohlemacher, Wissenschaftszentrum Berlin für Sozialforschung, Berlin 1993, p. 10.s

Figure 2

Die Flut steigt – wann sinkt das Boot?

The tide rises — when will the boat sink?
Nearly every minute a new asylum-seeker

„Deutsches Essen schlecht"

"German food bad"
Asylum-seekers on hunger-strike

Deutsches Mietrecht

German landlord and tenant law
Pensioner must leave to make way for asylum-seekers

Einer kam als Jürgen Klinsmann

One came as Jürgen Klinsmann
Swindling asylum-seekers and
their rotten tricks

Amtmann Müller: Was mir Asylbewerber so erzähler
Ich Asyl, ich Johnnie Walker

Senior civil servant Müller: What asylum-seekers are telling me:
Me asylum, Me Johnnie Walker

Figure 2 (continued)

Family must take in asylum-seekers

"Asylum, Asylum!"
Now they're coming as tourists

Asylum-seeker forced German woman into marriage
Violated, beaten with waterhose, dragged into mosque

False asylum-seeker slaughtered 9 women

One would probably not expect much better from a tabloid like the *BILD-Zeitung*. But even *Der Spiegel*, a major weekly news magazine, comparable to *Time* and *Newsweek* in the US, used horrifying front-covers. They showed a flood of foreigners storming 'the ark', Germany (Figure 3) and coming in through the gates (Figure 4).

In the five-month period from May to September 1991, in nationwide representative surveys, the proportion of the German population that spontaneously deemed the immigration issue to be 'the most important problem' in Germany, rose from about 10 per cent to 80 per cent. The figure for those who were worried about the issue never dropped below 40 per cent for another two years (source: ZDF-Politbarometer). Why? I think it is safe to say that the media's coverage of the issue contributed significantly to its standing in public opinion.

II

To understand how the press, radio and television help to raise public concern, it may help to consider five steps in the process whereby an issue becomes a crisis:

(1) The initial step consists in demonstrating that, somewhere in society, there is a *significant gulf between norm and reality*. What the mass media typically do, as in 1992-93 in Germany, is to make their audience aware of troublesome *events*, incidents which indicate a gulf between norm and reality. So, the headlines used as examples above suggested, for instance, that there were criminals among the refugees—a violation of a norm. But it was still not a *significant* violation—which it has to be if it is to become a problem.

(2) That is why single events have to be put in a wider context or 'universalized'; 'framed' is often the term used. In this way, troublesome incidents are no longer seen as deplorable but isolated cases. 'The more asylum-seekers there are, the greater the chance of finding a criminal among them', might suggest an isolated case, perhaps deplorable enough, but not a problem. Plane crashes are often depicted by the media as tragic but somehow non-problematic events. Sometimes, however, the media convey a wider concern. A single plane crash or, more often, a series of plane crashes may be seen as a problem of 'airline safety', for instance. Or, single cases of bribery and corruption may lead to a perception of 'government corruption'. What happened in 1992 and 1993, as far as the research shows, is that the media 'universalized' the events depicted in the above headlines as a coherent issue, namely that 'German immigration policy' had gone wrong.

Figure 3: *Der Spiegel*, 9/9/91: 'Refugees. Emigrants. Asylum-seekers. Onslaught of the poor'. Used with permission of *Der Spiegel*.

Figure 4: *Der Spiegel*, 6/4/92: 'Asylum. The politicians fail'. Used with permission of *Der Spiegel*.

(3) Another element of crisis-creation relates to the *urgency* of a problem. What should its priority be on the public agenda? Once placed on the public agenda, the urgency is determined both by the *intensity* of the gulf between norm and reality, as well as by its *prevalence*. 'Intensity' increases with the importance of the values that are threatened—for example, if the problem is considered not only bothersome but also dangerous. 'Prevalence' grows with the number of people involved or who should at least be concerned about it. The *BILD* headlines above, for instance, increased both criteria of urgency: 'something bad is happening to retired people in Germany and to normal German families who have to give up their homes because of refugees. But this development is even more threatening because asylum-seekers are killing women or forcing them into marriage'.

   All in all, the urgency of an issue is typically increased by the cumulative effect of various factors related to the way news is reported: the involvement of prominent people, a judgmental tone, the portrayal of innocent victims, geographical or cultural proximity, a clear-cut cause-effect relationship, and a view of the 'dynamics' of the problem—it is suddenly getting worse. The more these factors come into play, the more urgent the problem seems.

(4) The media may convey an idea of how simple or complicated an urgent problem is, and this itself will influence the public's proclivity to action. A problem can be 'killed', its position on the public agenda 'deflated', simply by declaring it important but intractable. The reason for this is simply that public attention is evanescent—it will not linger too long over issues that seemingly cannot be dealt with successfully.

(5) Providing impressions of the *prospects* of a solution is another area where the media can have an impact: 'Is it probable that an urgent problem that *can* be resolved, *will* in fact be resolved in time?'

How do these elements combine to create a crisis? Imagine a problem that is portrayed not only as serious but also as very urgent. In addition, there would appear to be a very simple, easy remedy for it—but those in charge do nothing about it. Fatal conclusion: '*We*, the people, have to resolve it.' This is how *revolutions* develop.

The German refugee issue of 1992 and 1993 contained all five elements. The way it was portrayed ensured that it had a very high news value. The problem was considered very urgent. The solution seemed at hand: 'Simply close the borders, keep them out, send them home.' But obviously nobody was doing anything about it. To say the least, all the ingredients of a highly explosive situation were present.

III

Frequently, media coverage not only tells a society how urgent a problem is, and whether it may be resolved, but also conveys an idea of how popular certain solutions are. During 1992-93, there was a perception that it was not unusual to use *violence* to resolve a problem that officials seemed to ignore. Ordinary people were taking action, and somewhat understandably so. Perceptions like this may initiate and accelerate a 'spiral of silence,' a process in public-opinion formation suggested by Elisabeth Noelle-Neumann, a well-known German mass-communication researcher (*The Spiral of Silence*, University of Chicago Press, 1993). She postulates a reciprocal relationship between the perceived climate of opinion and people's willingness to speak out. Once dramatic, even violent, solutions to 'the refugee problem' (such as: 'Throw them out!') become increasingly audible, even visible, then people who disagree begin to be silent in public whenever the topic comes up. They hesitate to articulate their views, to speak up. Noelle-Neumann claims that the reason for this behaviour is our deeply-rooted fear of being isolated socially, of being regarded as foolish or old-fashioned.

This kind of silence in public reflects not only a deplorable lack of courage, but has also quite dangerous side effects. Others get the (false) impression that this standpoint cannot be a popular opinion because nobody speaks up for it. In large societies where citizens are forced to rely on institutional sources of information, the mass media are important conveyors of such impressions. Thus, they can silence people or encourage them to speak up. Noelle-Neumann calls this process a 'spiral' because the more people fall silent or the more the media ignore a certain opinion—and thus create an impression of silence—the more the notion spreads that this conviction is losing ground, leading to the silencing of even more people.

This theory may explain some calamitous courses of history like that of the Third Reich: although they may have opposed the regime, people spoke out less and less, in part because they did not find their opinion reflected in the media, and thus—involuntarily—supported the notion that opposition to Hitler was dwindling.

To counter what they regarded as a disastrous process in public opinion in 1992, hundreds of thousands gathered with candles and silently marched or formed a chain in many German cities. These 'candle chains' early in 1993 were designed to reassure the peaceful majority of Germans that they *were* still the majority. Up to then, a person might have felt: 'If a foreigner is being threatened, it would be foolish to get up and do something about it, because I would be on my own.' Even if the effect of these candle chains were only short-lived, quite a few foreigners might have been protected by the impressions the marches were conveying.

IV

What was the media's role in the processes described above? Is it a matter of concern for journalists? Note that the impressions conveyed did not have to be *invented* by the media. Most of the time, media in democratic societies do not really make up events. But they do *select* and *present* the news, and not always autonomously: they may be used by people and institutions as a means of pursuing their own interests. In any case, whatever the *ultimate* source of the *media's* information, in most cases the media are the *immediate* source of the 'pictures in our heads' of the 'world outside' (Walter Lippmann). Certainly, one has to admit that German media spokespeople were correct in their somewhat naive way of defending themselves in 1992-93. 'The media', they claimed, 'were only reporting the truth and nothing but the truth.' And, indeed, their stories were mostly correct: there *were* criminals among the 300,000 refugees of 1992; the number of asylum-seekers *was* increasing; there *were* complaints about German food.

Indeed all the other requirements of the *Pressekodex*, the code of ethics for German journalists, were fulfilled as well: dubious methods of gathering information were not used: the confidentiality of sources was not violated; advertising and reporting were kept strictly separated; there was no invasion of privacy; religious feelings were not hurt; bribes to get information were not used. There was not even (and this was particularly interesting) 'an inappropriately sensationalist depiction of violence and brutality'. Most of the *BILD* headlines and most of the coverage in other newspapers and other media did not deal with violence and brutality at all.

Was truthful reporting enough, however? Wasn't there another dilemma, a moral one? Certainly, it was not the familiar dilemma involving privacy on the one hand, and public interest on the other—as in the case of Princess Diana, for instance. Nor was the moral dilemma between easy lies and a harmful, dangerous truth. Nor did it concern the dilemma of staying independent of one's sources, on the one hand, and having access to information, on the other. Instead, the dilemma arose on account of the harmful consequences for society brought about by the reporting and presentation of facts because of its connotations of self-censorship. This is a particularly intricate problem, one that cannot be easily resolved by traditional journalistic professionalism.

Journalists are typically trained to use craftsmanship rules, professional standards and guidelines such as: 'Be truthful'; 'Events are newsworthy if prominent people are involved'; 'Negative news is more important than positive news'; 'Events closer to home are more relevant than those happening in far-away lands'; 'Sudden processes are more newsworthy than slowly developing ones'. This is what journalists typically learn and what they typically apply in their daily routines. Given the pressure under which journalists often work, these routines are not only functional, but are also reassuring.

Resorting to those old rules of news selection and news presentation seems even more necessary and reassuring nowadays because journalists feel that the complexity of issues has increased. This does not mean to say that they have in fact become more complicated than they were, say, four hundred years ago. But the idea has spread that things are more complex. A second development supporting this reliance on traditional rules is that the larger a social system gets—and journalism now is a large system within society—the more 'self-referential' it becomes. Journalists often rely on the judgment of their peers, who also follow the same traditional rules of news selection and presentation.

V

In principle, there is nothing wrong with this power of television, press and radio to set the agenda for public discourse. This is what media are for in complex societies—to help direct public opinion. But this power requires a greater consideration of the moral dilemma posed by the effect on the audience or readership that the continued use of traditional news-presentation criteria may have. Resolving this dilemma is not easy. It requires what German sociologist Max Weber (1856-1920) called *Verantwortungsethik* ('the ethics of responsibility or accountability') rather than *Gesinnungsethik* ('the ethics of conscience'). *Gesinnungsethik* states: 'I act correctly as long as my *intentions* are good. And as a journalist I cannot go wrong as long as I follow the rules, such as being truthful in my reporting and focusing on negative events.' *Verantwortungsethik*, on the other hand, is more demanding. It is customarily required of doctors, architects and lawyers: they are held accountable for the consequences of their work. Applied to journalists, it means they have to take responsibility for what happens to their sources, to the people they report about, and finally to their audience. The first two groups are fairly well protected: the law, as well as codes of ethics, cover the rights of sources and the privacy of individuals. The audience, however, is not similarly protected.

To behave *verantwortungsethisch* toward the audience, it is not enough to be truthful in reporting. Sensitivity and care, and a sense of proportion and balance are required. Even if a report is completely true as well as important according to news criteria, journalists cannot leave it at that. There is still something more they have to consider. I wouldn't go as far as the Council of Europe in its 1993 resolution on 'The ethics of journalism'. This says that 'the media have a moral obligation to defend democratic values: respect for human dignity, solving problems by peaceful, tolerant means and consequently to oppose violence and the language of hatred and confrontation … the media must play a major role in preventing tension and must encourage mutual understanding, tolerance and trust.' It implies that the media are not only supposed to be *responsible* for the consequences of their reporting but that they also have to *fight* for something. In my view, it would be enough if the media tried to be more responsible for their actions, if journalists considered the way in which truthful and important news should be presented to their audience.

Such an attitude means nothing less than a paradigm shift: journalists and the media, as owners of certain communication rights, would have to waive some of those rights in favour of the audience, as the other owner of communication rights. This paradigm shift can only take place—and that is what makes change so difficult—if at least three requirements are met that would *enable* journalists to take more responsibility for their actions:

(1) The first requirement is *knowledge*. Training journalists to take on such responsibility goes beyond the classic subjects, such as writing and reporting, doing interviews well and applying the traditional news criteria. It goes beyond knowledge of the political system and other such subjects. It requires knowledge about the *audience*, and about the possible *effects* of media reporting.

(2) Also necessary is *time*. Journalists can only act responsibly, can only have recourse to criteria beyond craftsmanship rules, if there is time to think about the possible effects, to consider moral dilemmas.

(3) The third and final requirement is *permission*. This means that journalists have to be *allowed* to act more responsibly by their colleagues, by the owner of their media organization, by the company.

In the meantime, journalists could begin to do something which is very simple but effective: they could show a little more modesty. Why is it that one rarely reads in a newspaper such humble phrases as: 'This is how I experienced the event I'm describing, how I saw it. This is the best I can do, but it's only a *picture* of the world'? Perhaps this is asking a lot, because it goes against the old professionalism depicted above. It could, however, be the key to a *new* professionalism, a professionalism of modesty, service and accountability to the public.

Beyond the balance sheet:
the responsibilities of media owners

CLAUDE-JEAN BERTRAND

Constantly you hear complaints about the sorry state of the media. Actually, they are in better shape than they have ever been—but not good enough. And improving them is not a minor issue, like improving the coffee in the US or the trains in England: the fate of mankind depends on it—since there can be no survival without democracy and no democracy without a quality press. The need is to improve quality. When some major incident happens (like Diana's death or Clinton's indiscretion), quite a few people (unfortunately) talk about the need to pass restricting legislation—while others talk about the need for 'media ethics'.

I personally prefer the term 'quality control' because the concept is more inclusive and not so loaded with moralistic connotations, which irritate some people—and, after all, a corporation as such cannot have a moral sense. Also the term has positive connotations for every group involved in social communication: for media users, it implies a better product; for professionals, it means higher credibility and prestige; for owners, it smells of profit, in the Japanese fashion. Lastly, quality control implies action, not talk.

What does quality mean in the media field? I believe it means 'good service': to serve the public well, the public in general or one's particular public. To serve the public well, non-specialized media like newspapers, must assume all their functions. Meaning what? In order of decreasing importance: watch the environment, i.e. give a full and accurate report on what's going on; serve as a forum and as a mediator, so that the various groups in the population talk with each other and reach the needed consensus; supply people with an image of the world outside their personal experience (and not just the ugly side of it); transmit culture from one generation to the next, i.e. teach what (within the group) is done and not done; help people pursue happiness, i.e. entertain them—which is what most people expect from media; lastly, move goods by carrying advertising.

To serve the public well requires that journalists be as autonomous as possible from the powers-that-be, economic and political, which are the two major obstacles to fulfilling the missions of the media. Media owners (especially when that means thousands of share-holders) want media to be profitable. To that end, the easiest way may seem to be to offer the public easy stuff, simplistic entertainment and infotainment, the media equivalent of prostitution and drugs. This is what US media, even some of the most renowned, seem to be doing these days. As a well-known US columnist wrote:

> With honourable exceptions, American newspapers, magazines and television are today mainly concerned with stories and gossip about stars, including athletes and public figures, with backstage film and television reports and with promotional material on films and television programs.[1]

As for politicians, they look upon media either as tools to be used for their own purposes—or as threats to their power that must be shackled. Hence, they are very much inclined to pass restrictive laws, even the 'free enterprise freaks' among them (of the Reagan, Thatcher type), usually with the excuse that they are obeying an angry public opinion.

In my view, the only efficient long-term strategy to avoid both types of interference is for the media to obtain and keep the trust of the public. There are two ways, to be used together: one is to be responsive to its wants and needs, the other is to be responsible to it: to render accounts to media consumers. That implies finding out what it is that the public wants and needs; then producing and delivering it, then making sure that the public is satisfied.

How do you do it? One common answer is you get good journalists, and you watch whether the public buys and keeps buying your publication or keeps listening to or watching your broadcasts. That is a little simplistic—especially in the case of monopoly (which exists nearly everywhere in the provincial daily press), or national oligopoly (as in Australia with Murdoch and Black).

I suggest we have a closer look at the issue and the participants. There are six groups of people involved in social communication: media consumers, media professionals, media owners, media advertisers, and other business leaders, political decision makers, judges and media regulators.

When consumers feel the need for media to be reformed, they will appeal to legislators and regulators (especially in Latin countries), to journalists and radio and television producers (more commonly in the US). People do not normally turn towards business leaders, be they media owners or not. Why not? They believe they are only interested in making money. They believe they are not supposed to be interested in anything but making money, espe-

---

[1] William Pfaff in the *International Herald Tribune*, 18 December 1997.

cially the managers who often nowadays are outsiders hired to make the firm prosper.

On the contrary, I have come to believe that media managers are crucial to the improvement of media quality. For one thing, some owners have proved that they were motivated not by greed only but the desire to serve the public well. A few examples: the Astors in Britain in the days when they owned the *Times* and *The Observer*—or Thomson who spent millions modernizing of the *Sunday Times* and then *The Times*. Eugene Meyer who transformed the mediocre *Washington Post* after he bought it in 1933, and the Grahams after him—or Otis Chandler who did the same to the *Los Angeles Times* in the '60s. Such progress is generally brought about by appointing the right people in the newsroom, by setting a general policy and by deciding to spend the needed funds (or not seeking tainted money),

Actually, every businessman who owns a newspaper or broadcasting station, as opposed to a shoe factory or a candy store, should be aware, or be made aware, that he is in charge of a vital public service, and as a citizen should feel a special social responsibility towards the population.

To some extent, media controllers have an obligation to see to the ethics of their media simply because they are legally responsible for what is published. Everywhere in the world, even in the US with its famous (but mythical) First Amendment, there is democratic legislation restricting freedom of speech, for good reason. Those laws overlap with media ethics—and have awful teeth: a violation can cost you a million pounds, or several million dollars.

Last but not least, media owners should see to the quality of their product or service because it pays. If well managed, a quality medium earns more money, in the long run. Look at the *New York Times* or *The Economist* or more generally the growth of Britain's serious dailies since World War Two as opposed to the decline of the popular press: between 1946 and 1996, the 'heavies' increased their circulation by 92 per cent and the gutter press went down by 27 per cent.

It also pays in increased prestige and influence: before World War Two, it was common to compare the (*Manchester*) *Guardian*, which had a circulation of less than 50,000—and the popular dailies whose sales the press lords were pushing up to 2 million by all means and, by doing that, were losing most of their political clout.

Owners can have a terrible influence: look at what somebody has done to the London *Times* in recent years and what the same somebody did to the whole British popular press after he bought the *Sun* from the Mirror Group and turned it into a sensational rag. Yet conventional wisdom holds that the individual journalist is the one who commits all the sins. He/she can kill a story for money, or can libel a VIP, or can invent a story to get his/her by-line on the front page (like Janet Cooke at the *Washington Post* in 1981 who had to give back her Pulitzer prize). However, I think those are relatively minor sins, I mean, as compared to what media do: like ignoring the dangers of tobacco for 30 years, like giving unions and strikes a bad image over a hundred years, like systematically publishing interesting little items instead of focusing on important issues.

When the journalist misbehaves, he/she often has been pressured into doing it. After all, he/she never takes the major decisions, like to cover or not to cover some event. Being a salaried employee, he/she cannot easily refuse an order. So, not much can be done on a regular basis by journalists, not much can be achieved by unorganized consumers or by isolated outside observers like academics, *unless* they have the approval and support of media owners.

What do media proprietors or controllers need to do? They need to decide to hire well-educated journalists, instead of training office-boys on the job in small weeklies, as was done in Britain for so long. And they need to fund the training: media firms must generously help journalism-schools and finance their research, as they do in the US, directly or via foundations.

They need to make it possible for their journalists to do their job properly by providing enough staff, and relying less on wholesalers, like the Press Association in Britain. Some years ago, I was amazed that a decent daily like the *Minneapolis Tribune* took the AP story for an incident at a country fair twenty miles away. Adequate means includes salaries: quite a few Latin American journalists could not survive without two jobs (or more), one being with government or with a firm that they are supposed to cover—and not requiring much presence, if any. And controllers should make no unethical requirements, like demanding that a new shopping centre be written up, or like giving the fall of the Berlin Wall less air-time than the Kerrigan-Harding case (a conflict between two US ice-skaters). Media owners can make it clear to their staff that there are rules, written or unwritten, and that they must be respected—or else. Codes of ethics need teeth and experience proves that journalists are not good at chastising each other.

That leads me to my central point. Concern over media quality (according to me) also involves setting up a number of 'media accountability systems' (MAS) like having an in-house code of ethics, with a hierarchy of sanctions (both of which must have been debated with the staff), or appointing an ombudsman or organizing a local press council, etc.

At this point, I would like to say a few words about the MAS themselves, a list of which is given at the end of this chapter. The concept (as I use it) is very wide and so a little hazy: a MAS is any non-governmental, non-State, means of inducing newspeople to be ethical, that is to say, to serve the people well. It is a means of external moral pressure, as opposed to internal moral pressure (that of an honest person's conscience) and to external physical pressure (like that of police and courts). Those two were used for centuries but now the first is of little help when facing a conglomerate, and the second has been too often abused by enemies of media freedom.

Obviously just one MAS cannot do much, but a loose network of MAS could have great influence, especially if combined with competence and dedication on the part of newspeople, by which they obtain support from the public, voters and advertisers, and thus wield quite a lot of power. Moreover, if ethics (a personal or professional set of rules and duties) yields to 'quality control', then media owners and controllers can weigh in efficiently.

From experience, it seems that, faced with a MAS, they adopt different attitudes. They can accept it, and publish correction boxes, have a large 'Letters to the Editor' section and select mail critical of the newspaper.

But quite often they do not accept them: some (especially in the old days) rejected them all out of hand, like the publisher of the *Wall Street Journal*, who claimed it was his newspaper and he could do what he wanted with it and if people did not like it, they could stop buying it. French newspaper owners have never endorsed the '*charte des journalistes*' drafted by the journalists' union in 1918, one of the oldest codes in Europe. And they have never seriously discussed a press council. Only *Le Monde* has an ombudsman now. Some publishers opposed *journalism reviews* in the US by threatening to fire any of their journalists who contributed to the local one. In St Louis (Missouri) the very respectable *Post-Dispatch* blacked out the *St Louis JR* for over ten years. On the other hand, some editors sent encouragement, funds, even pieces to be published.

They can encourage them, with or without money. Take codes of ethics again: if a code is endorsed by management and, as quite often happens in the US, is included in the hiring contract—it obviously has much greater impact. Take readers' or viewers' associations: media controllers cannot be involved in the creation of them—but they can opt to listen (or not listen) to them: as was the case when a group of citizens created a press council in Hilo on the big island of Hawaii. And they can opt to give them publicity or not.

Better still, media owners can initiate MAS, like opinion surveys, like panels of readers or viewers, like local press councils. In the US, except for the six so-called Mellett councils (initiated by a union and managed by academics), all were started thus, from the first in 1950 at the Santa Rosa *Press-Democrat*, whose owner organized a monthly lunch with a group of eminent citizens to listen to their grievances. Actually, history shows that the staff is often more hostile to MAS than management: the appointment of ombudsmen has generally been opposed by newspeople and was decided by management—but the opposition was such at the French daily *Libération* that none was ever appointed.

Wherever they have been tried, MAS have given satisfactory results. Yet, they are rare, except for national or regional press councils, even in the US, where almost all of them have at some point existed. In the US there are about

30 ombudsmen for 1,600 dailies, 7,500 weeklies, 12,000 radio stations and 1,500 TV stations, and at least 2,000 consumer magazines.

What's the problem? I shall try and explain by listing the criticisms made of MAS and the obstacles they meet—apart from the fact that in no profession do people like innovations, especially when they jeopardize positions of prestige or power. So, for instance, nearly all press councils were set up in response to parliamentary threats. But that is not the whole story.

At both extremes of the political spectrum, there is opposition to press freedom. The only way to make the media serve 'the nation' or 'the people' is to own them all or to apply force. Ethics and MAS are seen as inventions of naive democrats.

Left of centre, social-democrats tend to look upon MAS as a PR ploy to avoid regulation: any effort on the part of media to be ethical can only be cosmetic. Right of centre, ultra-liberals present ethics and MAS as a communist plot against freedom of speech and free enterprise. Codes are of the same despicable nature as laws and regulations. Conservatives in general see ethics and MAS as a disguise for anti-media leftist militants: actually, in the US the most vocal critics are on the Right.

Cynics say ethics and MAS are useless: good media knew what was right before—and the bad media don't give a damn. Actually most journalists are neither good nor bad: they can do with guidelines and with the external moral pressure of peers. Realists find reality too complex and diverse for a three-page code to be helpful. The journalists are always in too much of a hurry to go and dig in a big fat book of rules. Besides, they have personal concerns such as to keep their job, get promoted, be influential and famous.

As regards the enforcement of rules, journalists do not expose or punish each other; media users are ignorant, unorganized and feel powerless. As for the owner himself, he often thinks the law is enough and a MAS is a violation of his right of property. When such an owner accepts a MAS, it is for PR reasons. I suspect that some owners also fear that MAS might be the sign of a slow revolution in the media world: a movement towards the participation of both producers and consumers. Media people in general are conservative: no more than other human beings do they like change. So strong pressure is needed for them to accept reform. Most efficiently, it has to be the threat of governmental action.

Though they have been elected by no one, nor had their competence tested by entrance examinations, many journalists feel endowed with superior grace. As high priests of information, they find it very hard to acknowledge their mistakes. Though they keep exposing decision-makers for various sins, they themselves find it very hard to take criticism. Fragile egos, probably. The profession closes ranks against any external criticism: the code (1954, revised 1986) of the International Federation of Journalists contains a last clause claiming that 'a journalist will accept only the judgment of his peers to the exclusion of any other'. But even the criticism of peers is not easily tolerated. Dog does not eat dog: media rarely criticize each other—nor do journalists, in public.

There are also objective obstacles to the setting up of MAS. One is the status of the journalist, an employee who can be displaced, demoted, fired if he does not obey orders. He/she would only be able to disobey if protected by the law, by unions, by the public—or by a quality-oriented policy set by the owner.

One obstacle could easily be swept aside: ignorance. Everybody, even outside the media, has heard about ethics, but many people, even inside the media, have never heard of what I call MAS . And the cause is that media have never worked at making them known. Actually, not so long ago, even ethics was taboo.

Two major obstacles to the development of MAS cannot be expected to yield to training, negotiation or experience. For one thing, some MAS can be expensive, if they are to do their job well, i.e. fast and visibly.[2] Journalists have no money to spare. Outside the US, there are few foundations. And it is considered better not to ask the State—although it is done in Finland and Germany (to finance the press council), to everybody's apparent satisfaction.

Actually, MAS are a good investment for whoever aims at improving both the quality of a medium and the image of a firm in the eyes of government, courts and public. But some owners do not want to help: why should they pay to yield power and be criticized? Others cannot afford to: they cannot, for instance, forbid freebies and junkets because they cannot cover such expenses.

Up to recently, I believed and I preached that to improve media service, there should be a clear division between media businessmen in charge of managing the company profitably, and media professionals in charge of providing the public with the needed information and entertainment.

I have changed my mind: now I believe that media owners/controllers/managers must play an active role in making media responsive and responsible through quality control. The main reason is that those people have the power to strangle or stifle the MAS, since they can provide, or withhold the publicity and the money needed to make a MAS successful. A MAS can be set up without them, but the evolution then is despairingly slow. Time is running out. It is crucial that media improve faster. The 'social responsibility' concept was introduced in the US in 1947: fifty years later, relatively little had been achieved, except the acceptance of the concept. So now all means must be used—and media owners are a very powerful means.

2 An ombudsman, for instance, needs to be a experienced, respected journalist, obviously well paid. A Press Council can only operate properly, fast, and assume all its tasks (like media monitoring) if it has a comfortable budget.

THE MAS
MEDIA ACCOUNTABILITY SYSTEMS

MAS could be classified according to the following four basic approaches but most actually use more than one:

- criticism, the oldest method, the easiest and most common.
- monitoring, now indispensable because media products are extremely numerous and short-lived—and because what media don't do is more important than what they do.
- public access to the media, needed for the feedback and because every group in the population must be able to correct or provide information about itself.
- training, the long-term solution to most media problems: the education of both professionals and media consumers.

Some MAS consist in a text or a broadcast programme:
- very visible correction boxes.
- pro-and-con opinions presented on all important public issues.
- letters to the Editor and Open Forums.
- on-line message boards and forums for immediate feedback.
- accuracy and fairness questionnaires, mailed to persons mentioned in the news[3] or published for all readers to answer.
- codes of ethics which media professionals have discussed and agreed upon—with, preferably, input by the public.
- regular media sections in newspapers and newsmagazines—or programmes on radio and television.
- journalism reviews, local or national, devoted principally to media criticism (e.g. the *American JR*).
- books written by professionals or by expert observers to expose media failings and recommend improvements.
- movies and television series dealing with media, sometimes critically, like *WKRP in Cincinnati* or *Lou Grant*; or a satirical programme like the daily *Les Guignols* on the French Canal Plus.

Some MAS consist in individuals or groups:
- in-house critics, 'staff review groups'[4] or 'contents evaluation commissions' (like those established by Japanese dailies as early as the '20s) to scrutinize their own newspaper for possible violations of ethics.

---

3 what *Globo* does systematically in Rio de Janeiro. **4** monthly rotating panels of journalists acting as a grand jury on newsroom issues.

- media reporters who keep a critical eye on a whole sector of the media industry and report on it to the public; and, when the occasion warrants it, courageous whistle-blowers.
- press ombudsmen, paid by a newspaper or broadcast station to deal with complaints from customers; and an ethics coach operating in the newsroom.
- liaison committees set up by media and some group with which they may occasionally clash, e.g. the legal profession or the police.
- citizens appointed to the editorial board.[5]
- local press councils, regular meetings of professionals from the local media and representative members of the community.
- regional and national media councils (composed of representatives of media owners, professionals and citizens), created by the media both to adjudicate complaints by media users and to defend press freedom against governmental threats.
- special quality control projects by media-related groups, like labour unions, professional associations, NGOs (like *Reporters sans frontières*).
- consumer associations, especially associations of media users, using awareness sessions, mail campaigns, opinion polls, evaluations, lobbying, even boycotts.
- the '*société de rédacteurs*', an association of newspeople, which usually owns shares in the company they work for, and has a voice in the setting of editorial policy.[6]

Similarly, the employees who own their medium.[7]
- the, even rarer, '*société de lecteurs*', an association of readers which buys shares in the capital of a medium and demands to have a say, even very small, in the general policy of the company.

Lastly, some MAS are processes:
- the crucial MAS: higher education.
- the further education of working journalists, through one-day workshops, one-week seminars, six-month or one-year fellowships at universities.
- internal awareness programs to increase the attention of media workers to the needs of citizens.
- regular opinion surveys; and, better, surveys of panels of citizens after they have been briefed by experts and have debated a given issue.
- the regular encounter of newspeople with citizens in some kind of press club or on the occasion of town meetings.

---

5 as at the Portland *Press-Herald*. 6 The first to attract attention was that of the French daily *Le Monde* in 1951. 7 like the *Peoria Journal-Star* since 1984.

- non-commercial research, done mainly by academics, often in 'media observatories' or foundation-funded think-tanks, on such topics as the perception of media messages by the public or the contents of media or the absence of contents.

Newspapers, standards, litigation: is there a better way?

CONOR BRADY

Some of you may be familiar with the works of a genre of British sociolo-gists in the 1960s and 1970s who undertook some then ground-breaking examinations of some of the influential institutions in British society. They especially took an interest in institutions for which the man or woman in the street had an ambivalent attitude, a love/hate approach if you like.

One in particular, a gentleman called Ben Whitaker, I recall, developed a metaphor to describe the relationship between the community and the police which I've always thought has some resonances also for the relationship between press and community. He likened the relationship between the police and citizen to that between sheep and sheepdogs. The sheep need the sheep-dogs to protect them and guard them—as a democracy needs a free press to guard its integrity but they desperately resent them when they get a nip on their own flanks.

I don't think he ever got around to newspapers—in fact I believe he became a member of parliament instead—but I would like to think that if he had done so and if he had isolated and described the emerging relationships between the British people and their press in the 1960s or 1970s, the rise of Mr Rupert Murdoch and Mr Robert Maxwell might not have been so assured. And some of the tabloid elements of the British press might not have quite descended to the standards they have reached in the 1990s.

He might have described the curious interaction between newspapers and their reading public who simultaneously wish to enjoy the pleasures of voyeurism while expressing moral indignation over it. There's a splendid vignette in Tom Stoppard's play *Day into Night* where a young lady, embar-rassed by, I think, some adverse publicity concerning one of her friends in the columns of the *Daily Telegraph*, utters the wonderful lines: 'Of course I'm all in favour of a free press. It's the bloody newspapers I can't stand.'

Because of our proximity, our shared language—and because they sell on our doorsteps—we tend to draw first comparisons between ourselves and the British newspapers. That can limit our horizons and block out our awareness of how they do things in other countries; smaller countries, with compara-ble populations, such as the Scandinavian ones. We could spend a long time arguing as to whether our standards here are better or worse than in the UK and it would not be very productive. For my money, when they deal with issues of privacy they are generally worse than our most raucous tabloids. When they're good, as many of their serious, well-resourced broadsheets are—they can often have much to teach us and the rest of the world about good journalism.

What we share with UK newspapers I suggest is that, perhaps more so than with newspapers in other countries, we are caught in the same bind of ambivalence with the public. They want us and they read us in great numbers. Though there are myths about this; one myth being that the Irish are among the greatest newspaper readers in the world—in fact on a chart showing newspaper circulations per thousand of population we come number 23 out of 40 developed countries.

The relevant figures nonetheless are impressive. Irish newspapers sell more than 570,000 copies each day and almost 680,000 on Sundays. Almost 900,000 weeklies are sold and almost 400,000 free newspapers are distributed. It's difficult to argue that there isn't a buoyant market for Irish newspapers. Notwithstanding this, I believe, our readers have in many respects a poor opinion of us. They do not trust us especially. They often don't believe us. And they generally support the notion that when we get it wrong and we're brought into court, we should get a good hammering.

Our own view, as newspaper journalists, of the reading public is often no less ambivalent. After all, that public pays our salaries. We would have no *raison d'être* without them. Our colleagues in marketing and circulation departments think about them a great deal, of course. They have to because they are the lifeblood of their trade. But as journalists and editors we don't always seem to accord to them the priority in our thinking to which they should be entitled.

Part of that is probably grounded in a healthy unwillingness to define our role merely in terms of what the readers say they want. But more of it, I believe, is grounded in the instinctive sense of those who operate any powerful institution that they are best left alone to get on with it—that the people whom it is designed to serve are at something of a nuisance and better kept at arm's length.

Maybe I'm wrong in this, but one person I know who is heavily involved in the voluntary sector said to me recently that it's a good deal easier for the citizen to get to talk to a cabinet minister or an archbishop than it is to talk to a newspaper editor.

I think that when we talk about publishing law in Ireland—and God knows, we talk a lot about it—when we talk about litigation and whether there should be a better way for newspapers and aggrieved citizens to sort out their differences—I think that we in the newspapers have to ask our-

selves some searching questions about our own responsiveness, our own willingness very often, to square up to our own mistakes and our own short-
comings.

However, I'm running a bit ahead of what I want to say on that. First, I
would like briefly to describe the body of existing publication law insofar as
it affects newspapers as well as tracing very briefly the history, over recent
years, of the various attempts to achieve reform.

Irish publishing law has remained unaltered for approximately forty years.
It was drawn up for a different country, a different time, a different society. It
reflects an era in which social mores were restrictive and authoritarian, in
which conventions of speech and commentary were timid and conservative,
in which authority figures and those in public life seldom had to endure a word
of public criticism or feel themselves called to account. It reflects an era in
which the newspapers themselves were seldom little more than polite gazettes
of daily life in a strictly-ordered, socially-stratified, homogenous and con-
formist society.

In that society legal proceedings for libel were a rarity. And when they did
take place, the relevant jurisprudence was itself grounded in caution and in
concepts from the antique. No apology could be issued by a publisher which
did not constitute an admission of culpability, thus leaving only the scale and
size of damages to be determined. The burden of proof lay entirely on the
defending party with proceedings starting from the assumptions that the published material was untrue and that the complainant had been damaged. The
law provided for no distinction between a libel which might have been per-
petrated inadvertently and one which had been pursued wickedly or mali-
ciously. And no element of mitigation could be claimed through any attempt
or endeavour by the publisher to withdraw, or clarify the material complained
of or to balance it with a contrary view or with additional information.

Not one whit of this has been changed, as we stand here, two years short
of the millennium. It's not for want of trying on the part of the newspapers, I
assure you.

In 1987 the National Newspapers of Ireland (NNI) began a process of dialogue with the Government and with the legal authorities to effect an overhaul of the law. A report was commissioned from two accomplished legal schol-
ars, Prof. Kevin Boyle and Ms Marie McGonagle, both of the law department
at University College Galway. Their exhaustive report, detailing the short-
comings in publishing law and demonstrating why it was failing to serve either
plaintiff or defendant, was finally presented in 1988 to the then Attorney
General, Mr John Murray SC.

Mr Murray decided to refer the matter to the Law Reform Commission
and, in due course in 1991, the Commission, under the chairmanship of Mr
Justice Ronan Keane, presented a comprehensive and potentially far-reach-

ing report. While it did not accept all of the arguments put forward by the NNI or by Boyle/McGonagle, it did, nevertheless, urge the overhaul of many of the more archaic aspects of the law.

That report gathered dust on the shelves of successive Governments and Ministers. It was claimed that due to a shortage of qualified personnel it was not possible to assign anyone to draft a suitable bill in response to the Law Reform Commission's conclusions. Finally, the NNI, after discussions with the Department of Law Reform, decided to commission a former parliamentary draughtsman, Mr Marcus Burke, to draw up a specimen bill—effectively discharging at its own cost that which should properly be the business of the State.

That bill was presented to the then Taoiseach, Mr Albert Reynolds, in 1994. Looking back on it, there was of course a profound irony in presenting that document to a Taoiseach who was himself going to set new records in suing newspapers—including my own—and accruing very large sums in damages through a series of actions.

Needless to say, there was no action on the bill during Mr Reynolds' period as Taoiseach. Perhaps, in retrospect, we ought not to have been surprised. Where we were surprised—and disappointed—was in the period during which Mr John Bruton was Taoiseach, in partnership with Mr Dick Spring and Mr Proinsias de Rossa. Repeated attempts to get the Minister for Law Reform, Mr Mervyn Taylor, to present the Bill—or a version of it—to Dáil Eireann fell on deaf ears.

We did get one significantly positive response from that Government in the wake of the collapse of the Irish Press Group. In 1996 we had the Report of the Commission on the Newspaper Industry, set up by the Minister for Trade and Industry Mr Richard Bruton. That report, in turn, urged the overhaul of publishing law—as well as a range of other measures designed to strengthen the industry. But there matters stand. Contacts continue between NNI and the present Government. I understand that some hopeful indications are emerging that at long last there may be some action. If so, it will be very welcome. But after twelve years one is cautious not to allow one's hopes to run too high!

I can't make anything more than an inspired guess at what the Government may think of doing. What we would like and what we believe we might have, realistically, at this time, is the right to publish an apology without prejudice, some changes in the rules governing lodgments in court and perhaps some recognition of the concept of inadvertent libel—the genuine error made in good faith and in spite of a journalist or editor having taken reasonable care.

In earlier discussions with previous administrations, it was made clear that there would be an expectation of some quid pro quo from the newspapers. Suggestions were made that the newspapers might put in place some regulatory body to deal with complaints from the public, perhaps something along the lines of a press council or a press ombudsman. And there have been suggestions of a code of practice to protect the citizen's privacy.

Whether these suggestions are to be resurrected remains to be seen. But it seems to those in authority, if we get measurable progress on our requests, that we should also be willing to consider what we can do, ourselves, to diminish the frequency of libel proceedings, to enhance our own standing with the general public and to create structures and procedures by which aggrieved individuals can have redress or satisfaction without having to go through the costly and slow processes of the law.

That doesn't seem unreasonable to me although I believe we should be very wary of ceding ground on possible privacy laws. It should be noted that the British have just this week set their face against such a development, notwithstanding the frequent intrusions of the press into the private lives of public individuals.

I believe it is wrong that a citizen should have to go to law to recover his or her good name as a result of something which has been published erroneously or carelessly in a newspaper or broadcast on the airwaves. We could go some distance, I believe, to address this sort of problem. It requires no great feat of the imagination to visualize the sort of structures which might be called into being or the sort of measures which might be taken by publishers, by editors and by journalists—without any government intervention or initiative.

These are the sort of measures which, I would suggest, might be taken by any service or industry which is anxious to maintain its own standards and to maintain positive and favourable relations with the people it is supposed to serve. These are the sort of measures, I would suggest, which we in the newspapers should be implementing for their own sake, for the sake of our own professionalism and reputation and regardless of whether the Government of the day has some reform proposals in mind.

Irish newspapers play a pivotal role in the political and public life of this society. One has only to consider the sequences of events which in recent months have led to the uncovering of successive scandals in public affairs to realize that were it not for the newspapers much of what we now know would never have become public knowledge at all.

Notwithstanding this, I believe that in certain respects, some Irish newspapers have to take a hard look at themselves, at their procedures, at their standards, at the way they discharge their responsibilities to the community they serve. I believe that what I say has application to publishers and proprietors, to editors and editorial managers and to journalists themselves.

There are model proprietors, scrupulous editors and conscientious journalists. But there are also proprietors who do not always display a full understanding of the obligations which attach to ownership of a newspaper. There are editors who too often seem to make no serious effort to apply any consistency of standards or values in validating material for publication. There are journalists who are indifferent to some of the most fundamental tenets of our craft—to seek out the other side, to hear what they have to say and to give them a fair showing; to differentiate between information which is given off the record and on the record; to take on board views and information which may run against the grain of a story or report; to check—and not to assume— the basic facts of what they submit for publication.

I must quickly add that I recognize the many excellent and accomplished journalists who practice our craft . I acknowledge the work which has been done down the years at the Dublin Institute of Technology—formerly the Rathmines journalism course—and in particular I applaud the vision of Dublin City University (DCU) in providing both bachelor-level and master's degrees in journalism.

But the great majority of practitioners in Irish journalism, at whatever level, receive no professional training whatsoever after their basic induction course. In-service training—other than purely technical instruction—is virtually unknown in most newspapers or publishing groups. Proprietors and editors have been in dereliction in not providing for continuing training. And journalists have been in dereliction in not demanding it. Again I would suggest we must look at other small countries in Europe for a headline. Danish journalists, for example, have a continuing programme of in-service training which actually forms part of the contractual relationship between journalists and proprietors.

Many of those who work in Irish newspapers remain wholly in ignorance of the growing body of professional knowledge which now informs their counterparts in the United States and throughout Europe. Journalism is not an exact science nor does it require that its practitioners acquire a great body of professional knowledge as in the case of medical doctors, or lawyers or engineers. But it is amenable to academic or methodical inquiry. It can benefit from the development of contextual principles . It benefits from reflection, from consideration of its successes and failures. It functions better if it has a clearer understanding of its role and purpose in the society it is seeking to serve.

There are many areas in which journalists in developed countries increasingly recognize the need to work to accepted standards and to try to adhere to what might be described as best practices. What ought to be the working ethics of journalists? What channels of inquiry or practices are legitimate and productive? What standards and criteria ought to be applied for the validation of news material which is destined for publication? What are the responsibilities of one journalist to another—the headline-writer to the reporter, for instance? How does one best train journalists who will be editors?

I would suggest that where the general public still has a positive view of newspaper work it tends to be informed by media representations such as *All the President's Men* or the *Lou Grant* TV series. But very often, what happens in some Irish newsrooms, I believe, can be quite different.

Those of you who remember *All The President's Men* will recall that even in the 1970s, *Washington Post* journalists had hard and fast rules as to when a source's statement was on or off the record. And they had hard and fast rules that reports could only be submitted for publication when supported by two independent sources.

Personally, I think the latter criterion is a nonsense. One good source may be more reliable than half a dozen bad ones But I would suggest to you that we could easily run up a list of supposed news-stories, published over any given period in this jurisdiction, where there has been no source at all!

I have seen—and you have seen—too many headlines on lead stories which ultimately go back to rumour, or indirect and uncheckable information, or which have been culled from another publication—almost invariably without attribution.

I can pinpoint too many instances in which stories that have come our way at the *Irish Times* have not been published because they could not possibly be verified or corroborated, but which have appeared almost immediately in other newspapers. I am left with the conclusion that these stories have gone to publication without what I would consider adequate validation or corroboration—or that our reporters lack the forensic skills of their counterparts elsewhere!

However, over the years I have become familiar with another remarkable phenomenon—finding *Irish Times* reports and, indeed, even on occasion *Irish Times* pictures on the front pages of another newspaper's late editions.

If some editors are happy to present as their lead stories that which comes at best from second-hand sources, if some journalists are happy to turn out copy which may bear no trace of an attempt to be fair, if some publishers are content to preside over this, invoking the principle of non-intervention, then we can hardly be surprised if the public at large, over time, comes to quite negative conclusions about their newspapers and about the people who work in them.

If newspapers treat their readers with contempt, they will, in turn, be treated with contempt by their readers. I believe the history of the Readers' Representative desks in Irish newspapers is illustrative.

At the beginning of the decade, with the publication of the Law Reform Commission's document on libel, the NNI felt it would help the climate of

relationships between newspapers, the public and the powers that be, if newspapers took the initiative in establishing a Readers' Representative desk in
each newspaper publishing house. There was nothing radical or new about
this idea. Readers' Representatives have been operating in US and European
newspapers since the 1970s.

Accordingly, newspaper groups throughout the State appointed a range of
individuals to act as quasi-ombudsmen on behalf of the readers, examining
complaints from the readership, seeking to ensure corrections or clarifications
where necessary, sometimes—if nothing else could be done—at least explain-
ing to baffled readers why certain things appeared or did not appear in the
newspaper.

Today, I believe it is fair to say, the *Irish Times* alone among Irish newspapers continues to promulgate the service of the readers representative desk. I
hesitate to say the office has been abolished elsewhere but if it exists in most
other Irish newspapers it does so as a minor adjunct to someone else's main
job, operating as a closely-guarded secret and without any apparent channel
or point of contact for the reader to operate through.

Some of my colleagues in other newspapers tell me the system declined
because it was not working. I don't accept that. The Readers' Representative
at the *Irish Times* satisfactorily resolved more than 90 per cent of the complaints or observations which were lodged last year. I believe we had something in the order of 900 in the year. I believe there were a number of con-
tributory factors to the decline—or demise—of the Readers' Representative.
I believe many proprietors and many editors, in their hearts, did not support
the concept and only went along with it because they saw it adding to the creation of a positive atmosphere in which concessions might be forthcoming on
libel. I believe many journalists regarded it as a nuisance, had no faith in it,
saw it as toothless and felt they could afford to ignore it. And I believe, as it
became clear that there was no imminent reform coming on the libel front,
that the minimal commitment to the concept which existed just faded away.

Today, insofar as many Irish newspapers are concerned, we are once again
back to the situation where an aggrieved citizen or reader, if he wants to make
a point, or seek redress, or if he simply wants to put the record straight, has
nowhere to go as of right, short of the law courts. He or she may be lucky and
get through to the editor, or a sympathetic member of his editorial or administrative staff. But we know, from countless anecdote, that he or she is far more
likely to get through to a harassed reporter or sub-editor, to be dealt with at
best brusquely, at worst rudely and seldom getting a considered response,
much less a satisfactory result. It is not always possible for a newspaper to fully
satisfy the demands of aggrieved readers. But they are surely entitled to a polite
response and, at least, to know that someone has listened to them and considered their point of view.

So, is there a better way than litigation? Yes, of course there is. But I believe that those of us who work within newspapers should not sit back and expect the Government to transform the situation for us. We need reform of the law to allow us to function fully as news media ought to function in the 1990s. We need reform of the law to enable us to see off the quick-buck merchants who see an opportunity for easy money in some infelicitous phrase or in some unhappy juxtaposition of words and pictures.

But apart from this, in some measure we have remedial options in our own hands. As editors and journalists we have ground to make up *vis-à-vis* best international standards in training, in work-practices, in developing some consistency of standards, in developing a clearer understanding of our role in the society we serve.

If we have action from Government on libel, it may well be that there will be a requirement for the establishment of some sort of newspaper ombudsman, someone who will bring an element of independence to the adjudication of complaints against newspapers.

Frankly, I think it will come as a massive culture-shock. Irish editors and Irish journalists, in too many instances, are not responsive to complaints. We are highly sensitive to any hint of criticism and we are slow to import into our own thinking the standards of openness and accountability which we so readily urge upon others. I believe the virtual disappearance of the Readers' Representative concept speaks volumes.

Have I any positive suggestions? I could make one straight away. I believe that proprietors, editors and journalists can make a common response, if they are so inclined. Provision might be made for advanced or in-service training, perhaps in tandem with some of the educational institutions. We have basic training for journalists and a Master's course at DCU. These could form the basis of new, expanded curricula to include study of journalistic decision-making, newspaper leadership and management, newspaper ethics and work-practices. Training links could be developed with some of the many excellent centres in Europe and the United States which seek to professionalize journalism at all levels. I qualified this prescription by saying that this could be achieved if there is the inclination or disposition to do it. I don't believe that all proprietors have such an inclination. I don't believe that all editors have it. And I don't know that all rank-and-file journalists are likely to give it the priority I think it deserves. Perhaps I am unduly pessimistic in this. Maybe everybody will prove me wrong.

We have fine traditions of newspaper journalism in this country. The quality of writing is generally high and, on occasion, may qualify as fine literature! The standards of reportage, of analysis and of presentation are generally good. Irish journalism is in thrall to no party, or church, or powerful interest group. Even where titles are linked through proprietorship to large companies, individual journalists and editors have rarely failed to defend and maintain an ethos of independence. As journalists we value the truth and we value our own professional detachment.

But we should not be unwilling to explore ways in which we might do better.

Can codes of conduct work?

ROBERT PINKER

THE PRESS COMPLAINTS COMMISSION—
ITS ORIGINS, CONSTITUTION AND REMIT

The British Press Complaints Commission was established in 1991 as a successor to the old Press Council which had acted as the newspapers' regulatory body for nearly forty years. By the end of the 1980s, the Press Council was in serious difficulties. A small number of newspapers were repeatedly ignoring its adjudications and advice. There was mounting public concern about press intrusions into the private lives of individuals. It seemed very likely that the government of the day would step in and appoint a statutory body to regulate the press. In the event, it set up a Departmental Committee under the chairmanship of Sir David Calcutt to review the situation and advise on future options. The Calcutt Committee reported in 1990 and recommended that press self-regulation should be given one last chance to prove its effectiveness.

The industry responded swiftly to this challenge. It established a Press Standards Board of Finance to raise an annual levy with which to establish the new PCC, a Code Committee of industry members to draft a Code of Practice and a committee to appoint the chairman and the members of the new Commission. The early days of the PCC were often fraught and difficult. The future of self-regulation remained very much in the balance throughout the first two or three years. Nevertheless, we survived and, I would argue, the last few years of the Commission's work marks a record of steady improvement and success.

The Commission currently consists of sixteen members, the majority of them laymen, working under an independent chairman, Lord Wakeham. The PCC is a self-regulating body entirely independent of both the industry and government. It receives and deals with complaints falling within the remit of the industry's Code of Practice. This Code is kept under continuous review by a Committee made up of working editors. The Code of Practice is the bedrock of the Commission's work but its provisions are *not* set in stone. The Code Committee and the Commission have always been responsive to changes in public values and concerns and to changes in technology and practice within the industry. Over the years since 1991, new modifications and additions have been made to the Code with regard to such issues as the use of listening devices and long-lens cameras, the definition of 'private property' and 'public interest', the prevention of jigsaw identification in child sex cases and the procedures to be followed in dealing with hospital authorities.

The tragedy of Princess Diana's untimely death has given all of us cause for considered reflection on the effectiveness of press self-regulation in the United Kingdom. The industry, through the consultative procedures of the Code Committee and the Commission, has responded swiftly and, we believe, effectively. The whole process of the review leading up to the introduction of a revised Code of Practice has taken less than sixteen weeks.

This speed of response was possible only because the consultative mechanisms were already established, because the Code has always been kept under continuous review and because many of the issues of direct relevance to the circumstances of Princess Diana's death, notably privacy intrusion and harassment, were under consideration at the time.

The introduction of the revised Code of Practice should not therefore be seen as a panic response to a worsening state of affairs. It is a considered response to a uniquely tragic event.

What kinds of sanctions does the Commission impose on publications that breach the Code? As a self-regulatory body, it does not impose fines or require payments of financial compensation.

When a complaint is upheld, the offending newspaper or periodical must and does publish the Commission's critical adjudication with due prominence. The Commission also publishes its own adjudications, both the upheld and rejected complaints and also a note of every complaint received. In 1993, the industry agreed that the Commission should have the facility to ask a proprietor/publisher to consider disciplinary action in appropriate circumstances where the breach in question is considered gross or flagrant. To underpin the progress we have made in recent years, more and more publishers are writing a requirement to abide by the Code into their contracts and conditions of employment.

THE EFFECTIVENESS OF SELF-REGULATION

How effective have these procedures been? So far, the newspaper industry has given 100 per cent support to the Commission and its administration of the Code. No newspaper or periodical has refused to publish an adverse adjudication. Some critics of the Commission are unimpressed by such evidence of universal compliance. They argue that publishers and editors are, unsurprisingly, more than content with a range of sanctions that cost them nothing in financial terms.

I sometimes wish it were possible for such critics to see the correspondence or eavesdrop on the telephone conversations between Commission staff and editors when an adverse adjudication is imminent or after it has been made. Over 80 per cent of all the complaints received which raise a possible breach of the Code are resolved informally to the satisfaction of the parties involved through the intervention and mediation of the Commission's officers. Most of these complaints are resolved in favour of the complainant.

The remaining 20 per cent that go to full adjudication do so, either because there are *prima facie* grounds for believing that an informal apology would not be sufficient, or because the editors concerned are convinced that they have not breached the Code and that a formal adjudication will vindicate them. They argue their case with vigour. They do not like losing and they do not like having to publish a critical adjudication which reflects adversely on their professional judgment and competence. Nevertheless, they always comply.

In summary, the greater part of the Commission's work is concerned with conciliation and the informal resolution of disputes. The remaining part of its work is concerned with formal adjudications which may result in the public censure of an editor. Both procedures work effectively because the entire industry supports the Code of Practice. They do so for two main reasons.

Firstly, the Code belongs to the industry. The Code Committee consists of a small group of editors who have kept the Code under continuous review since they first wrote and circulated it to the industry for endorsement. All changes in the Code, whether they are major or minor in character, are made subject to the approval and support of the industry. Their compliance is voluntary but, nonetheless, it is binding. And that, in essence, is the strength of the self-regulatory system. Secondly, the industry has a manifest interest in making self-regulation work. If it were to fail, they know that the government would intervene and impose a statutory system.

There are, however, some other measures of effectiveness in addition to the 100 per cent support which the industry gives to the Commission in its enforcement of the Code. Unlike a legal system of adjudication, the only cost falling on the complainant is the price of a postage stamp. 86 per cent of all the complaints about press intrusions into privacy which the Commission received between January 1995 and August 1997 came from so called 'ordinary' members of the public as distinct from celebrities, other high profile people and organizations. This ratio, I suggest, would be reversed in any alternative legally based system without the provision of legal aid.

It should also be noted that the average time taken to resolve these complaints from their date of receipt to their date of completion was thirteen weeks. Once again, it is difficult to imagine an alternative statutory system delivering this speed of service and response—at no cost to the citizen.

THE PATTERN OF COMPLAINTS

How widely known and used is the Commission by members of the public? The overall number of complaints has increased over the years from just over 1,500 in 1991 to just over 2,500 in 1995. In 1996, the number rose to just over 3,000. The greater part of this increase is attributable to the fact that the work of the Commission has become much better known to member of the public. The Commission's information literature has been revised and improved. The key pamphlet, *How to Complain*, has been translated into a range of minority languages and a Text-phone service has been introduced to assist the deaf and hard of hearing. The Help-Line telephone service received an average of 135 enquiries a week in 1996.

Almost seven in ten of all the complaints received in 1996 were raised under what were then the first three clauses of the old Code which covered matters relating to accuracy, opportunity to reply and Comment, Conjecture and Fact. The proportion of complaints received under the old Clause 4 which covered intrusions into people's privacy accounted for 13 per cent of the total. In summary, the greater part of the Commission's work—over 80 per cent of all complaints received—has so far fallen within the terms of four clauses of the Code. In quantitative terms, cases of unjustified intrusion into people's privacy are not numerous. Nevertheless, invasions of privacy can be deeply hurtful to the individuals affected. Their effects can extend to innocent relatives and friends, and the are just as hurtful to ordinary citizens as they are to public figures. Privacy was the issue that caused the government of the day to establish the first Calcutt Committee of Enquiry and privacy continues to hold a salient significance in the work of the Commission. This is why the Commission appointed one of its members to have a special responsibility for all procedural matters relating to privacy intrusion.

SELF-REGULATION AND THE EUROPEAN CONVENTION

The incorporation of the European Convention on Human Rights into English law will have important implications for the future of self-regulation. I would like to focus on three issues of current concern—the extent to which the British system of voluntary self-regulation will be able to coexist easily with these new legal provisions; what these changes will mean for the future status of the Commission; and whether they will result in the judiciary developing a common law of privacy by the 'back door'.

On the first of these issues—coexistence or, rather, compatibility, I can see little or no reason for concern. It seems to me that the principle of self-regulation is entirely compatible with the principle of subsidiarity which has always been a central element in the movement towards European integration since the European Commission made its submission to the Tindemans Report on European Union in June 1975.

The principle of subsidiarity states that decisions should be taken at the lowest level consistent with effective action within a political system. Its purpose is to check and prevent the centralization of powers within a federal constitution. The origins of this principle, however, can be traced back to the papal encyclical *Quadragesimo anno* of 1931 in which it was deployed to protect the Church from unwarranted extensions of statutory authority. The same principle has equal relevance today in protecting other secular institutions from similar extensions and incursions.

In any event, the purpose of the European Convention on Human Rights is to protect individuals from abuses of power by the state and other public bodies that act in its name. Which brings me to the second issue of current concern—whether or not the Commission will be defined as a public body under the new legislation?

Article 8 of the Convention makes it 'unlawful for a public authority to act in a way which is incompatible with one or more of the Convention Rights'. The two key rights which have to be balanced against each other are 'the right to respect for privacy' under Article 8 and the right 'to receive and impart information and ideas without interference by public authority' under Article 10.

An editorial in *The Times* points out that the reference under Article 8 to 'one or more of the Convention rights' leaves a potentially dangerous area of ambiguity which might result in 'a court judgment based on only one of the rights laid down in the Convention'. It should not, however, be difficult to resolve this matter by an amendment to the Bill.

If, however, the Commission were to be defined as a public authority under the UK Bill, its adjudications would be open to challenge in the courts, and newspapers would be subject to interim injunctions in cases of privacy intrusion. As *The Times* observes, this new state of affairs 'would offer the powerful and those who would abuse their power many new and wide opportunities to impede investigative journalism'.

The Lord Chancellor thinks that the Commission is a public authority and that if it were legally recognized as such and were willing to add fines to its range of sanctions the judges would be less inclined to intervene. The counter-arguments to this view are that a system of fines would seriously damage our highly efficient conciliation procedures and thereby undermine the whole self-regulatory system. Editors would be far less likely to admit that they had breached the Code if such an admission left them open to heavy fines or litigation or a combination of both.

In a letter to the *Financial Times* the Commission's chairman, Lord Wakeham, has set out the case for excluding the PCC from the provisions of the Bill. First, he notes that no court has ever held the Commission to be liable to judicial review and that we have never accepted that we are liable. Secondly, he reiterates that the Bill is concerned with the rights of individuals against the state and not against other private individuals or organizations. On this ground alone the Commission, in company with all other voluntary and private organizations that are not part of the government and are not exercising statutory functions, ought to be excluded.

Thirdly, he lists the reasons why the Commission ought not to be defined as a public authority. It does not discharge any statutory functions. It does not receive any public monies. It administers a voluntary Code of Practice. It does not have any legal sanctions. And, it could be voluntarily dissolved tomorrow without regard to the wishes of Government or anyone else.

Finally, Lord Wakeham addressed the third main issue which I referred to earlier—are the courts likely to develop a common law right to privacy in the aftermath of incorporation? He points out that, so far there has been no collegiate decision on the part of the judiciary to do so. In this respect it should be noted that the new Bill will not, in itself, create a new tort of infringement of privacy. Individual citizens who want to sue a newspaper will still have to do so through the provisions of existing laws concerning breach of confidence, trespass, harassment and electronic bugging.

Nevertheless, such actions under English law can be very expensive and their outcomes are most uncertain. And judges will still have to balance the claims of Article 8 against those of Article 10 as they are incorporated into English law. For all these reasons, it is still my view that the ad hoc development of a common law of privacy is neither inevitable nor desirable.

In this event it now seems likely that the Bill will be amended to take account of most concerns. The Press Complaints Commission will be defined as a public authority but its new statute will include a safeguard which specifies that the grounds on which its decisions can be challenged in the UK Courts must be consistent with those which have applied in previous Strasbourg judgments. Two judgments have so far been sympathetic to the rights embodied in Article 10 with regard to freedom of expression.

In addition, the Press Complaints Commission's decisions will only be open to challenge in the UK Courts if it is deemed to have acted in breach of its own Code of Practice. Neither will the Commission be required to involve itself in any 'prior restraint' actions.

THE REVISED CODE OF PRACTICE

The public interest

The revised Code of Practice came into effect on 1 January 1998. The Commission's chairman, Lord Wakeham, has described it as the 'toughest' Code of its kind in Europe. It may be helpful if I start with some general comments on the new format which will set the specific changes in their broader context.

The old Code of Practice consisted of seventeen clauses listing a sequence of ethical issues which might give cause for complaint. The eighteenth clause set out the grounds on which a newspaper or periodical could invoke a public interest defence with regard to privacy intrusion, the use of listening devices, misrepresentation, harassment and payment for articles. Publications might go beyond the requirements of these clauses if they believed and could subsequently demonstrate that, in doing so, their investigations and reporting served the public interest.

The old Clause 18 specified the following grounds on which editors could invoke a public interest defence, namely, in:

I detecting or exposing crime or serious misdemeanour
II protecting public health and safety
III preventing the public from being misled by some statement or action of an ndividual or an organization

The first two exceptions listed under the old Clause 18 seldom gave rise to difficulties. It was, however, the third subclause that was most frequently and controversially invoked by editors as providing a *prima facie* public interest justification for intruding into people's privacy, using listening devices and so on. Editors, for example, claim, often successfully, that readers have a right to know when the public statements of politicians are misleading because they can be shown to be seriously inconsistent with aspects of their own private behaviour.

In the format of the new Code the public interest is set out, not as a clause, but in the form of a general bold-type statement. The old clause covering Comment, Conjecture and Fact has been subsumed with accuracy, leaving sixteen instead of seventeen clauses on specific issues.

Two important changes have been made to the wording and coverage of the public interest statement. In cases involving children, the Code now requires editors to 'demonstrate an exceptional public interest to over-ride the normally paramount interests of the child'. In addition, the number and range of ethical issues on which editors may invoke a public interest defence has been increased to include children, access to hospitals or similar institutions and the identification of innocent friends and relatives.

These extensions cover issues that have, in the past, caused editors to invoke what proved—in the event—to be a successful public interest defence. At the same time, the preamble to the Code reminds editors that they must honour its requirements 'not only to the letter but in the full spirit'. In addition, it should be noted that editors were recently warned by Lord Wakeham that, in future, the Commission would 'tighten up on the use of the public interest defence—by making its deployment and the PCC's judgment on it, more transparent to the public and politicians'. He stated categorically that the public interest defence must not be used by editors 'to drive a coach and horses' through the requirements of the Code. He also drew particular attention to the need to protect the interests of children and other innocent and vulnerable relatives.

Privacy

Important changes have been made with regard to privacy intrusion. The old clause simply prohibited 'intrusions and enquiries into an individual's private life without his or her consent'. It also prohibited 'the use of long-lens photography to take pictures of people on private property without their consent'. Both requirements were subject to a public interest defence.

The new clause states that 'everyone is entitled to respect for his or her private and family life, home, health and correspondence'. It also retains the ban on 'the use of long-lens photography to take pictures of people in private places without their consent'. Private places are now defined as 'public or private property where there is a reasonable expectation of privacy'.

The new clause, therefore, refers explicitly to some of the everyday aspects of privacy, including one's house, health and correspondence, which most people value highly and which have, in the past, arisen most frequently in complaints about intrusion.

As for the definition of private property, the Code Committee was faced with a difficult choice when it came to this part of its review. It could have set out a list of places that had to be treated as private. The list, however, would have been a long one but no matter how lengthy it had been, it would still have had to be open-ended. If past experience has taught us anything in these matters, it is to expect the unexpected.

Not too long ago, for example, we received our first ever complaint from a person who was approached for an interview just after she had entered a church. The editor put forward a public interest defence and, for good measure, argued that the part of a church in which people hang their coats is not properly part of a place of worship. We upheld the complaint on the grounds that no public interest was served by such intrusion and that, by all the criteria of commonsense and reasonableness, a church is a church full stop.

There is, I suggest, an inescapably subjective dimension to the concept of privacy. Furthermore, on the basis of past experience, every Commissioner knows how vitally important it is to take into account *all* of the specific circumstances relating to a particular complaint. There *may* be contexts in which photographing someone on a beach or the back of a taxi is defensible. There must, therefore, be some scope for the exercise of discretion on the part of the Commission. I am in no doubt that the Code Committee was right when it decided to word the definition of 'public places' in sufficiently general terms to meet the requirements of commonsense and civility while leaving scope for the exercise of discretion.

The industry's endorsement of this new wording confirms their confidence in our good faith and ability to exercise this new scope for discretion in a responsible way. For our part, we are confident that editors will continue to act in a like manner.

Harassment

The issue of harassment is closely linked to that of privacy. We may never know everything about all of the circumstances surrounding the death of Princess Diana. We do know that on the night of the tragedy her party left in some haste by the backdoor of the hotel in order to avoid pursuit and harassment by the paparazzi. Over the years, many other people have suffered harassment from a 'media pack' without any possibility of escape. If such people refuse to talk to anyone, the harassment can last for a very long time and, without the name of at least one of the newspapers or reporters involved, their complaint cannot be pursued by the Commission.

Some forms of harassment are collective and unintentional in character. Major tragedies like Dunblane and transport disasters are issues of manifest public interest that are bound to bring large numbers of the press and other media to the stricken location. In recent years, thanks to the co-operation of the industry and the work of the Commission, there has been a marked improvement in press conduct at the scene of major tragedies.

The death of the Princess, however, dramatically focused everyone's attention on the phenomenon of harassment as it affects the everyday lives of ordinary people as well as those of public figures. The wording of the new clause now includes the imperative 'must' and the phrase 'persistent pursuit' so that the key requirement reads as follows: 'Journalists and photographers must neither obtain nor seek to obtain information or pictures through intimidation, harassment or persistent pursuit'.

The new harassment clause also expects editors to ensure that their staff conform to those requirements and forbids them from publishing 'material from other sources which does not meet these requirements'. The Commission cannot prevent the paparazzi from taking pictures at home or abroad in ways which breach the Code. It cannot prevent private agencies from buying such pictures. It can, with the co-operation of the British press, stop their sale and publication in the United Kingdom.

Children

The clause on children has been substantially amended. It now starts with a new requirement, subject to the public interest proviso, that 'young people should be free to complete their time at school without unnecessary intrusion'. The old requirement that 'journalists should not normally interview or photograph children under the age of 16' has been toughened up. The phrase 'should not normally' now reads 'must not' do so.

A new subclause has been added which forbids payment to minors or to their parents or guardians unless it can be shown to be demonstrably in the child's interest. In addition, where material about the private life of a child is published 'there must be justification for publication other than the fame, notoriety or position of his or her parents or guardian'. Clearly, this new requirement will help to protect the children of royalty and other well known public figures. It will, however, also provide the same protection for the children of people who hold other kinds of public office like members of the professions, elected councillors and other officials. And it will do the same for the children of people who become subjects of criminal proceedings or other kinds of unwelcome public interest or censure.

The requirements concerning children involved in sex cases are made more categorical and the wording has been simplified. These requirements, all of which are directed towards protecting the anonymity of the children, remain unchanged.

Intrusions into grief and shock

One laudable change has been made to the clause concerning intrusions into grief and shock. The old clause simply required reporters to carry out their enquiries into cases involving grief and shock with 'sympathy and discretion'. There have, however, been a number of complaints in the past about insensitive reporting, notably from relatives and friends with regard to news items on inquests. The Commission has never involved itself in adjudicating on matters of taste and decency although it has occasionally expressed a collective opinion on such matters.

The Code Committee has, however, addressed the issue of insensitive reporting by adding the following sentence to the clause on 'Grief and Shock': 'Publication must be handled sensitively at such times, but this should not be interpreted as restricting the right to report judicial proceedings'. Not all deaths or suicides are matters of public or even personal regret and this fact applies as much to the columns of court and inquest reports as it does to those of the obituary notices. On the basis of past experience, however, it is clear that some seriously distressed people have suffered further unnecessary pain as a consequence of reporting that was unintentionally insensitive.

Other changes to the Code

Two other changes to the Code should be noted. The clause on accuracy—which has always been the subject of most complaints—now explicitly prohibits the use of inaccurate, misleading or distorted pictures as well as written material. This requirement takes account of picture manipulation abuses. The once separate requirement to 'distinguish clearly between comment, conjecture and fact' has been subsumed into the clause on accuracy.

And lastly, the clause on discrimination now includes 'mental illness and disability' among the conditions about which editors 'should avoid publishing details' unless they are 'directly relevant to the story'.

CONCLUSION

Taken in their entirety, these changes cover a very wide remit that goes beyond those parts of the Code that have a clear and direct relevance to the circumstances of Princess Diana's death. As such, they constitute both a defining moment in the history of British press self-regulation and one of the many stages in the continuous process of reappraisal, review and revision that is making self-regulation more and more effective as a key institutional part of a free society.

Representatives of the industry, serving as members of the Code Committee and the Commission, wrote the original Code and have kept it under review ever since. The industry endorsed and continues to endorse the Code. It is *their* Code and they have agreed to uphold it. The Commission enforces the Code as a completely independent body.

This unique division of responsibilities, based as it is on a principle of voluntary compliance, makes self-regulation the best kind of regulation. It protects the citizen from abuses of press power, it defends freedom of expression, and it serves the public interest. When these rights and interests conflict and when conciliation fails, the Commission adjudicates. Self-regulation is fast, efficient and accessible to everyone, rich and poor alike. We do not need more state intervention or more powerful sanctions than those we already have.

Cleraun, in close association with Opus Dei, is a study centre committed to fostering Christian ideals and character development. The Press Complaints Commission is concerned with ethical issues of a more mundane and secular nature. It attempts to reconcile the claims of three important principles that are central elements in the affairs of a democratic society—the right to freedom of expression, the right to privacy and the claims of the public interest.

None of these rights is absolute. Each of them is conditional on the others and is qualified by various legal and non-legal restraints. Freedom of expression, for example, is subject to the laws of defamation. Privacy may have its darker as well as its lighter aspects. And we can only grow up to enjoy and value the experience of our privacy in a context of social relationships. What counts as a matter of public interest is often a matter of debate and disagreement. It is also important to remind ourselves, in the context of the media, that the public interest is not necessarily synonymous with what happens to interest the public.

In the last analysis, however, the Press Complaints Commission administers a Code of Ethical Practice designed to ensure that, as far as it is possible, relations between the press and the public are conducted with a degree of civility and consideration. Voluntary compliance to agreed standards of conduct is the *sine qua non* of ethical behaviour.

It also happens to be the lynch-pin of the British press self-regulatory system. In the age of the Internet and an open global communications system, there is no other way of doing the job effectively.

The newspaper ombudsman:
public accountability or public relations?

ROBERT HEALY

Sometime in the late '60s, the era of the rise of feminism and protest of the Vietnam war, the offices of the editor and executive editor at the *Boston Globe* were taken over and a sit-in was established by a women's group called 'Bread and Roses'. The group had its beginning in New England during the industrial revolution when women worked the looms and machines in the huge textile mills of Lawrence and Lowell. Their working conditions were bad; their pay was worse.

These were not mill workers who sat in at the newspaper; they were a combination of up-scale career women and women who had attended the best of the Ivy league schools in New England and New York, the Bryn Mawrs, Harvards and Yales. There was little connection between these women and the original group of mill workers; only an adopted name and a reason to protest. For them it was a combined exercise of power and a statement for change of what was being printed in the *Boston Globe*. No one with any authority at the *Globe* even suggested that they be thrown out of the offices.

The product of the protest would be given a mixed review: the women wanted an end to sexist advertisements for films. Despite the First Amendment problem here for the advertisers, the women scored a compromise. The women wanted a column on the opinion page once a week, to be written ostensibly by one of them, to be edited by the group and the headline over the column to be written by the group. They won a partial nod on this.

They were told to produce the column first and the editors of the *Globe* would edit the piece for taste and accuracy and would be influenced by the suggested headlines. They never produced the column. As we suspected, opinion columns are almost impossible to write by a large committee. They simply could not agree on what to say.

What they did win was an ombudsman. The protest had a great impact on the newspaper's publisher who was thinking about a means to meet the public's protest and to learn what the readers did not like about the writing and editing of the *Boston Globe*.

The publisher liked the idea of an ombudsman. I was executive editor of the newspaper with responsibility over both the editorial page and the news operation. I thought it was a thoroughly bad idea. What were editors supposed to do if they did not represent the public interest? What would the great American editors, such a Ralph McGill in Atlanta or Joseph Pulitzer in New York and St Louis, think about an ombudsman imposed on their operation of their newspapers? Not much I suspected.

But the publisher owned the newspaper, set the news budget, hired and fired editors. Somehow he prevailed. We had an ombudsman. 'Bread and Roses', the women's protest group, had won a big one.

So what is an ombudsman? The word has a soothing quality and could almost be used as a mantra for newspaper executives who are worried about their sagging credibility with readers, according to a piece in the *Columbia Journalism Review*.

Actually 'ombudsman' is a Scandinavian word which in English means 'go-between' or 'intermediary.' The first ombudsman was appointed in 1809 in Sweden to handle citizens' complaints about government. Now ombudsmen can be found in government, hospitals, corporations, universities and other institutions. In the news business there is a world wide organization of ombudsmen which include members in the United States, Canada, Japan, Israel, Spain, Brazil, Sweden, Ecuador and Paraguay. I did not see any listed in Ireland. However I am not about to be a nine-month expert on Irish journalism. I will focus on what I know, American journalism.

The shape of the ombudsman in the American newspapers takes many forms and sizes. Some are outright stooges for their newspapers, leading the cheers for what they call great stories and the courage of editors in the face of adversity. While all that they write could be true, that is not what the job is about. The second is the technical ombudsman who catches bad grammar, misspelling and bad punctuation and basically critiques bad writing. While all that is not a bad idea, it, too, is not the function of the ombudsman. The third class of ombudsman operates as an outsider in a sense. He or she catches the real waves of criticism from the readers of a story, acts independently to check accuracy, speaks to the reporter and the editor who handle the story. Then the ombudsman puts together the criticism with the facts and writes a column which says something: the editors were wrong in handling the story, the reporter was overboard for one side or another and wrote a bad story, or the criticism was not valid and here's why.

Of course, the keys to good performance, independence and job security, come into play here. The person who is looking to be an ombudsman and runs a campaign for it generally does not deserve it. Just as not all police should be given a badge. And the person who takes the position as ombudsman must not be worried about getting fired the first time he or she roams out of the stable and writes that the editor has made a big mistake.

So job description comes into play. Some work for the executive editor, the managing editor or city editor. That doesn't work well. The line of authority should come down from the publisher who in most papers these days has direct control over the editorial page and its editor. That provides the ombudsman with independence to do the job, which is monitoring the news, feature columns, photography, and cartoons for balance, fairness and accuracy and to bring substandard work to the attention of the public, the news staff and the editors. A good strong contract for the ombudsman's reign also helps.

It is important to know that the subject of ombudsman goes beyond the person. It touches the very heart of the system—the people's right to know, freedom of speech and the press, the conflict in the US Constitution's Bill of Rights between the First and Sixth Amendments, the freedom of expression in the First and the right to privacy in the Sixth. It goes to the question of how much freedom there will be and where, how and by whom the brakes are applied.

But no matter how the role of the ombudsman is structured, it will not still the basic criticism of the press. It has been around too long. One of my favorite stories is that of a man named Lincoln Steffens, one of the early journalist muckrakers, who took on big city corruption in Chicago and elsewhere in the United States. In the 1920s he came to Boston at the invitation of the Good Government Association, or as the Irish American politicians called them the Goo Goos. The Goo Goos, white Anglo-Saxon Protestants who ruled Boston for generations, and the new Irish immigrants were anathema to each other. At the heart of the subject was who would govern Boston.

A Boston ward boss by the name of Martin Lomasney was promoting the mayoral election of James Michael Curley and the Goo Goos wanted Steffens to do a hatchet job on the Lomasney political machine, write a report which would be picked up by all the Boston newspapers and kill off the election of a Curley or some other product of Lomasney's machine. Curley was later elected.

After many months of studying and talking to the players in Boston's political machine, Steffens produced his paper for the Goo Goos. He wrote that if it was not for the political machines such as Lomasney's to redistribute the wealth of the Goo Goos, the ton of coal to the cold, the Turkey for the Thanksgiving day meal or the sweater under the Christmas tree, these same people would be throwing rocks. The targets would be the stores, the bank, the newspapers and insurance company windows. The Goo Goos, wrote Steffens, should be grateful they had a Lomasney political machine in Boston. It saved them from themselves and made the system endure.

Steffens then was kind of early ombudsman and, like some other ombudsmen who followed him, Steffens' report never saw the light of day in the Boston newspapers.

In 1947, the Hutchins Commission on Freedom of the Press, a group of notable non-journalists convened by *Time* magazine publisher Henry Luce, measured the press, found it wanting and levelled this grave warning: either monitor itself or be monitored by the government. The Commission wrote: 'One of the most effective ways of improving the press is blocked by the press itself. By a kind of unwritten law, the press ignores the errors and misrepresentations, the lies and scandals, of which its members are guilty.'

The commission's report was largely ignored by the press, as you might expect. Twenty seven years later when A. H. Rankin of the *New York Times*, one of the great reporters for that paper, suggested that newspapers appoint an ombudsman for the readers 'armed with authority to get something about valid complaints and to propose methods for more effective performance of the paper's service to the community', the message again got nowhere.

But by the '60s there were other forces at work for the ombudsman in newspapers. It was a combination of things. In the single newspaper cities, and there were more and more of them throughout America, the big newspapers were beginning to take on what had been some sacred institutions, untouchable until that time; the churches, the universities, big business and government. These large institutions did not roll over for the press criticism. They had the resources to tackle the press independently. Also in the large cities on both coasts, alternate media sprung up, publications such as the *Village Voice* in New York, the *Phoenix* in Boston. The alternate press was delighted in giving voice to any protest by any institution against the one big newspaper in town.

There were other influences. Seán MacBride was making speeches at the International Press Institute calling for the licensing of journalists. His major complaint was that Northern European journalists had misrepresented what was happening in the new countries of Africa and these countries should have the right to decide who was going to do the reporting. This sent chills down the backs of American journalists. There was also much talk of news councils in America. The news council in my judgment is a homemade censorship board.

Ben Bradlee, executive editor of the *Washington Post* during Watergate and President Nixon's resignation from office, saw the writing on the wall and became a supporter of the ombudsman. I might add, an unlikely supporter. But unlike the *Louisville Courier Journal* in Kentucky, the first newspaper to establish the ombudsman, the *Post*'s person not only answered complaints from readers and corrected errors but also commented publicly and many times critically on the paper's performance in a weekly column. Bradlee said going public was an essential part of the ombudsman's role. 'It prevents editors from sweeping anything under the rug. You have a representative out there who's saying, "Don't do that. You guys goofed. You fell short of your goals."'

There was then in the air an implicit message for the press: clean up your own house or government will do it.

But no one should think that the ombudsman is the ultimate medicine for bad journalism. Remember in most cases the ombudsman comes into play when the newspaper has made a mistake and is called on that mistake by the readers. A legion of ombudsmen and a bible of rules cannot take the place of the execution of a thorough reporter's work, well trained in the craft. That followed by the hand of experienced editors who can spot a bad one and insist on excellence.

No case says more about this than that of the *Washington Post*'s Janet Cooke, a facile writer, winner of a Pulitzer prize, who made it all up.

Bill Green was the ombudsman for the *Washington Post* at the time and he wrote a powerful 18,000-word report on Cooke's faked stories. Some said it was a triumph for ombudsmen because it was a complete and wrenching confessional of the *Post*'s mistakes. Cooke was a young black woman who had faked her credentials to get the job at the *Post* and had faked stories about children in the ghetto. They were written in such a compelling manner they literally made readers weep.

Robert Maynard, the late editor, publisher, and owner of the *Oakland Tribune* in California and a former *Washington Post* ombudsman, and also a black, said it was 'as much a failure of ombudsmanship as it was a failure of any other part of the system'.

Maynard said, 'People tend to say, "Gee, it took the *Post* by surprise; they didn't realize there was a problem until after the Pulitzer."' Well, that's not true. There were plenty of reporters and people in the community who had serious complaints about the story at the time it was published, but the ombudsman made no attempt to find out for himself whether there might be validity to those criticisms,' he told the *Columbia Journalism Review* at the time.

Bradlee responded to that in typical Bradlee fashion: 'That's bullshit,' he said. 'The case represents a failure on our part to check references on new employees, and a failure on our part to demand from reporters the degree of sourcing that we do now.' He's right. No ombudsman can or should be expected to flag the kind of mistakes made from the day Cooke came to the *Post* to the day her stories were published and her Pulitzer prize had to be returned.

What it shows, too, is the basic ambivalence about the role of the ombudsman. The role is still relatively new in American journalism. The ombudsman in the large newspaper is somewhat different from that of the smaller newspapers where the contact with the readers is always more direct with the editors. Nor has it had a great deal of growth among American newspapers in the last ten or fifteen years.

Were there lessons learned from the Cooke affair? You bet there were. I remember shortly after it became public, the American Society of Newspaper

Editors had its annual meeting in Washington. Bradlee had been scheduled on the program before the Cooke stories were published for an early morning session to speak on being a big time editor made famous by Robert Redford's *All the President's Men*. Most editors don't make the first call for meetings at 8:30 a.m. but this morning they were wall to wall in the hall. They licked their chops at the notion of Bradlee's confessional. Bradlee didn't duck it. With his publisher Don Graham at his side, he tackled the errors straight on. There was a lot of note-taking in the audience. Editors left the meeting with a laundry list for their staffs about how to avoid another Cooke affair, a laundry list neatly provided them by Bradlee.

There is, of course, another view about ombudsmen from that of Bradlee and Maynard, who basically supported the function. Robert Haiman, a former executive editor of the *St Petersburg Times*, called the system of ombudsman a sham. Once a supporter, Haiman was bitten by an ombudsman. In June of 1980 his ombudsman wrote a column questioning why three black journalists, and no whites, had been assigned to cover the race riots in Miami. The black reporters said their integrity in reporting the story had been unfairly questioned. Haiman agreed with them and ordered the ombudsman to publicly apologize or quit. The ombudsman quit.

Haiman told the *Columbia Journalism Review* at the time that when his ombudsman quit he had a talk with the telephone operators at the newspaper and he told them that when a reader had a beef with a story that the operator was to put the call through to the proper editor, sports if it was a sports story, city desk if it was a local story. 'And if someone calls and says who is the head son of a bitch, let me talk to him, I said you put that call on my line.' Haiman admitted that the editor of the *Washington Post* or the *New York Times* probably could not take all the calls coming to them but that did not mean that ombudsmen were necessary or right for all newspapers.

Anyone who thinks the reader is always right belongs in the circulation or subscription department of a newspaper. Readers hate trashy stories about sex and violence. What stories do they read? Stories about sex and violence. Readers know how to better edit the newspaper than editors; ask them to put their ideas on how the newspaper should be edited into writing and you never hear from them.

On the other hand, readers sense when they are not getting the straight stuff from a newspaper, they sometimes find errors that editors don't see or overlook, and they can be offended and even hurt by what they consider bad taste. That is where ombudsmen fill the bill.

Gordon McKibben, the *Boston Globe*'s ombudsman for a number of years, kept a running log of calls estimated at about 6,000 a year. He said he thought most callers were serious readers who had a genuine attachment to the newspaper and about half the calls of complaint start with an approximation of 'I like the *Globe*, have been reading it for 30 years but ...' And then they proceeded with their complaints.

'If any grand theme has emerged from the thousand of complaints,' he said, 'I have heard it is a concern about intrusion of privacy. I've heard it from many angles: Why did the *Globe* have to run a photo of that child playing, because child molesters can find him? Why did the *Globe* print a street address that might imperil the witness to a crime? Why did the *Globe* run that embarrassing photo? Why did the *Globe* give away the identity of an Alcoholics Anonymous member? Why can't the *Globe* follow through and prominently report the facts when a youth who is charged with a crime or an embarrassment is later found innocent?'

Those are all reasonable questions. But how about these two calls to the same ombudsman: Woman: 'Thanks to the *Globe* for publishing Spanish-language soccer reports.' Man: 'The *Globe* is pandering to foreigners by publishing stories in Spanish and I demand that you stop at once.' Where's the wisdom in that one for the editor?

In America today there is great focus on the media, television, talk radio and newspapers. The media has become a story itself. Reporters are assigned to write exclusively about the media. Talk radio in the United States is a disaster. They call themselves journalists and many if they were not on the public airwaves would be selling snake oil. They are pitch men and entertainers. The pitch men don't do interviews, they argue and when they don't prevail they cut off the person being interviewed.

And then there is television, where on many channels you can't tell the news from the entertainment. The trained seal comes to mind for the *John McLaughlin Show*, seen here in Ireland on NBC television. It is presented as a news show. Topics are serious and on the news. But John throws the ball to his seals and if they don't catch it just right, he cuts them dead. Just as an aside: I used to appear on that show once in a while until my wife said she was going to leave me if I didn't stop. Tim Russert of NBC's *Meet the Press* is another breed. It is a hard news show, with tough questions, but he gives the person being interviewed a real chance for a responsive answer, and I think that's really the difference between these two shows.

In this media jungle, newspapers are fighting for their role. They must retain credibility and the ombudsman is directed toward credibility with the folks who are buying the newspaper. The reader loves to see the ombudsman write about a fouled-up story, 'We were wrong, we just blew it.' But too many of those confessions and the newspaper has some trouble too.

I was in the newspaper business for 45 years and, believe me, with all their problems, most newspapers are much better now then they were when I began. The writers are better, they are better educated, the reports are better, the range of topics is much more extensive. The special, once-a-week sections on business, sports, science and health, living and the arts probably saved the large newspapers in America.

But the monopoly newspaper in a city, while generally producing a better product, has had its cost in the loss of trust of the readers. Newspapers must learn that there really is no monopoly in the media. Even where there is a single publication in a city. There are other voices; the all-news radio and CNN are real competition. And they must not try to be like television or radio because they cannot compete with them on the clock. They must bring to the reader a different dimension than radio and television.

In the department of credibility, newspapers must keep their news separate from opinion and opinion clearly labelled. If someone is writing an opinion piece on why energy prices are high and the writer is on the payroll of the oil industry, the reader should at least be informed of that fact. Newspapers should learn to be beaten on a story once in a while by television and radio in the interest of accuracy. Making mistakes on radio and television is not the same as in print. Accuracy, as any worthwhile ombudsman will tell you, is still number one for a newspaper.

And finally, newspapers have to learn to do what they do best, and do it better than radio and television.

Leaks to the media:
should the information always be used?

SEÁN DUIGNAN

I rather liked being called a spin-doctor. It conveyed an aura of being in control, pulling the strings, of being a cunning manipulator of media opinion, etc., instead of the reality, which was being confused, often panic-stricken, most of the time.

Leaking is generally regarded as the business of spin-doctors, and a somewhat dishonourable business at that—for example, nobody likes admitting to leaking—but, in my view, the practice *per se* is not particularly reprehensible. True, it is usually done for the most venal and self-serving reason, but I would still posit that, in the exercise of practical politics, it is also as natural, and unavoidable, as breathing. Certainly, as Government Press Secretary, I participated energetically and enthusiastically in the whole business of spinning, leaking, etc.

However, I wasn't good at it. Here's what I wrote, somewhat peevishly, in my diary after being outmanoeuvred for the umpteenth time: 'The key to leaking is to just do it, then blithely deny it, irrespective of speculation, accusation or even verification. In politics, it is not a "lie" to deny you're about to devalue your currency, even as you prepare to do it, nor, it would seem, to disclaim responsibility for leaking even when the whole world knows you're guilty. It's just business—*realpolitik*—and my only regret is that I'm just not as good at leaking as Labour ...'

Ah, poor Diggy, but I was a little sorry for myself the day I wrote that.* We were paranoid about Labour leaks around that time, regularly blaming the party, but, of course, we could never prove it.

It has been said that information is power. Certainly, getting it first, hoarding it, feeding it out—usually selectively, but sometimes fully—is an intrinsic part of modern politics. Lots of it is done purely to curry favour with individual journalists; also, of course, to make one's own team look good; to outmanoeuvre or embarrass one's opponents. It never has anything to do with openness and transparency.

---

* It may be pertinent, at this point, to mention that I tend perhaps towards heavy-handed irony, and that, notwithstanding the *Irish Times* gauging the above diary extract to have been in actual earnest, a measure of facetiousness should be acceptable on such a subject matter.

When John Bruton espoused just such openness upon being elected Taoiseach, I wrote that genuinely open government and natural political secretiveness, in my admittedly cynical view, would never be reconciled. You'll remember him saying: 'Government must be seen to be operating as if behind a pane of glass.' He actually meant it, but I immediately wrote in my diary: 'That'll be the day!'

In that regard, it's important to understand at least one element of the relationship between politicians and journalists, or rather how politicians think that relationship works. Something else I wrote at the time: 'The notion dies hard among politicians that they can have "friends" among the media. They tell you they know this can be done, because so many of their opponents have manifestly pulled it off, so why not them? Therefore, all they require is the right spinner/stroker with the right touch to massage the hacks into acknowledging their conspicuous worth. To this purpose, they cultivate a wide range of journalistic contacts, plying them with exclusive interviews, quotes, steers, leaks … and … almost invariably wind up in spluttering high dudgeon as the favoured ones bite the hand that feeds them.'

By the same token, leaking is frequently counter-productive. Certainly, the politician who thinks a hot piece of information, or even a classic beat, entitles him or her to everlasting gratitude is being most unwise.

That is for a variety of reasons. Journalists, by and large, don't need to be thankful. For example, information that reflects well on those who do the leaking, particularly if they are in power, is not really what their business is about. The name of the game, quite understandably, I suppose, is to expose whatever government may be doing wrong, thus underlining the watchdog role of the fourth estate, and the resultant biting of the hand that feeds it. But, then, who was it said?: 'You cannot hope to bribe or twist, thank God, the British (?) journalist, but, seeing what the man will do unbribed, there's no occasion to.'

Having worked on both sides of the fence, as poacher and gamekeeper, I am aware, not just of the mote in the eye of the politician, but also of the little peculiarities we (I'm wearing my media cap now) have as journalists. For example, the media insist on having it both ways on leaking; indeed, we award ourselves the most amazing latitude, being not just the enthusiastic recipients of leaks, even demanding such leaks at times, but having no difficulty whatsoever with maintaining this attitude at the same time as, say, the newspaper which employs us thunders denunciation of politically-inspired leaks.

It is as if the media right hand doesn't know, or doesn't want to know, what the left one is doing. Regularly, political reporters will make private pitches for use of sensitive documents—the more sensitive the better—pleading that the material should be given to them alone, rather than to any of their colleagues; and they see no contradiction between that and their editorial page denouncing such leaks. I suspect the people who write these editorials don't worry about it either. Invariably, of course, they only denounce leaks to other rival papers.

Incidentally, it may be useful to define what actually constitutes leaking, or rather what is not a leak. For example, one of the most notorious of the so-called leaks during Albert Reynolds' time was not one at all. That was the controversial publication of the Beef Tribunal report without consulting Labour. It was actually a full frontal attempt at a pre-emptive strike which boomeranged disastrously.

I would emphasise, too, that the vast majority of leaks do not achieve their objective. Historically, one of the earliest such efforts, I recall, was back in 1948. It involved then-Taoiseach John A. Costello announcing, in Ottawa, of all places, the Inter-Party Government's intention to declare Ireland a republic. Nobody has ever understood why he did it in the way he did—to steal Fianna Fáil's thunder?, to give two fingers to de Valera?, why in Ottawa?, etc. At any rate, the point is that his people leaked it in advance to the *Sunday Independent*, but it was so badly botched, that they didn't really appreciate what they had, and never properly used it. The whole thing, as Prof. Joe Lee wrote in his *Ireland 1912-1985*, was 'a shambles from start to finish, perhaps the most inept diplomatic exhibition in the history of the state'.

Jump forward almost exactly fifty years, and the even more botched attempt to damage Mary McAleese by leaking the contents of a conversation she had with a Foreign Affairs official on, shall we say, sensitive northern matters. Now, even by ruthless political standards, that was very bold indeed. It was calculated to destroy her as a presidential candidate.

But the upshot was that it had precisely the opposite effect, the Irish suddenly swinging decisively behind the McAleese campaign. Leaking is a bit like bomb manufacturing. It can blow up in your face.

Of course, some well-timed releases of information are successful. One I particularly recall is interesting, because it came not from a political source (at last not directly) but still spectacularly achieved what was intended. This was the release of the contents of an interview done with the late Brian Lenihan a few years before Brian contested the Presidency. He looked a certain winner until this explosive stuff was suddenly produced in the middle of the campaign. It stopped Brian Lenihan dead in his tracks; it cost him the election, and effectively ended his political career.

Of course, you can argue that it was not really a leak, rather more a conscience-driven act of civic rectitude, or take the opposite view that the interview was done on the basis of historical academic research, and that, therefore, the interviewer was actually obliged not to publish. Either way, it still fulfills the ultimate objective of the classic inspired political leak, destruction of the intended target.

Perhaps more related to this particular exercise, however, was the leaking to the *Irish Press* (during my time as Government Press Secretary) of the contents of an Irish position paper on what eventually wound up as the Downing Street Declaration.

It caused such pandemonium—'national sabotage' said Albert Reynolds; 'a vile deed' said Dick Spring—that a Garda enquiry was launched, and the recipient of the leak, Emily O'Reilly, was grilled by detectives for hours on end. Interestingly, O'Reilly did subsequently tell me a little of what happened. It was a man, she said. He gave her a copy of the document to peruse quickly, then when he felt she was too slow in taking notes of its contents, almost casually told her to hang onto it.

In a broader context, as tension increased between Reynolds and Spring in government, leaking became more and more associated with their manoeuvrings, and the bitter row over the appointment of Harry Whelehan, as President of the High Court, brought this to a dangerous pitch.

We were on our way to Australia after a huge cabinet row over Harry Whelehan. Quote from my diary: 'I told him (Albert) that I had talked to Labour before leaving, stressing the vital importance of keeping the cabinet row confidential ... Reynolds said: "Don't fool yourself ... they'll have it in the 'Sundays' (the Sunday newspapers)."' Three days later, on arrival in Perth, Western Australia, I wrote: 'Not a line in the Saturday papers ... maybe it'll be OK. Albert says "I'll believe it when I DON'T see it." We are snowed under in Perth with media attention. Ireland/Peace a big deal ... etc.' Within a few hours I was forced to add: 'Mary K (Mary Kerrigan, Fianna Fáil press secretary) rings to end the blissful illusion. Albert was right. They have it in the "Sundays". Labour leaking like a sieve ... to Emily, Olivia, Stephen, Gene Kerrigan et al. The story is Labour stopped the Taoiseach railroading / ramrodding Harry through in his usual arrogant fashion'.

The next paragraph is another excerpt from the diary, a day or two later: 20 September, 1994 Canberra—'We are overwhelmed by the extent of the Labour blitzkrieg. They are going all out ... Labour denying they are responsible for the spin [by that, I meant the leaks] but even the papers are commenting on the audacity of the Labour background briefings, with little or no attempt to disguise responsibility of Labour sources ...' And that, of course, goes back to my original theory about leaking. That one just does it, then denies it—certainly never admits it—irrespective of speculation, accusation, or even verification.

Of course, there were also Fianna Fáil (FF) leaks. Here's one that illustrates the importance of inside information and how to use it. During the ritual dance that Labour conducted with all parties before going into government with Reynolds, they timed the release of a list of demands to Fianna Fáil for the eve of Reynolds and his top ministers departing to Edinburgh for a hugely important EU summit on regional funding. This was calculated to prevent an early FF reply until after the summit. But pro-Fianna Fáil elements within Labour (pro in the sense that they wished to wind up in government with Fianna Fáil) had already leaked the contents to Fianna Fáil, so when the Labour document arrived, this was what happened. I subsequently wrote: 'Within an hour, even before the Taoiseach's plane took off, a considered 20-page response from Fianna Fáil was lobbed back over the Labour fence ...'

I go on: 'Mansergh's rapid-fire rejoinder was distinguished by its readiness to accept, word for word, in some cases, the Labour proposals ...' And I conclude: 'So, as the Taoiseach headed for Scotland, the mood aboard the government jet was: "Now, let Labour put that in their pipe and smoke it."' There's nothing a politician enjoys more than such a little stroke—'we were so clever weren't we?'—only, it probably didn't matter a damn; more likely than not, Labour were going to come into government with Fianna Fáil at any rate.

Then there was the famous Donogh O'Malley leak on free secondary education in the mid-Sixties. His was a classic use of prior leaking in order to ensure the desired outcome. O'Malley figured he probably would not get it through cabinet, certainly not past the Department of Finance mandarins, so he simply went over all their heads, directly to the public, via the media. He had it leaked, and the Government was swept along on the tide of public enthusiasm for the plan. It had no choice but to adopt the O'Malley plan.

There's also the curious case of the leak of a key document which arguably never existed. Reynolds and John Hume have differed over the celebrated Hume/Adams document which reportedly constituted the entire basis for the IRA cease-fire and inclusive peace process. Only nobody in Government ever saw it. At one stage, John Hume said he was about to hand it to Reynolds, and then he left for the United States. 27 September 1993 (diary): 'What's Hume up to? I have rarely seen Taoiseach and Mansergh so upset. Haven't a clue where he is ... we're getting reports from US that he has already given Albert the report, then that he'll give to him when he gets back. Mansergh says we've got nothing from Hume or Adams. Still, nobody here wants a public row with John. So I go on as if everything is perfect. What a way to make a living!'

7 October 1993 (ten days later): 'I keep telling corrs the report has "significant potential", that it will be "part of the process", etc. But I gather the "written" report is in the form of notes, i.e. practically back of envelope stuff ... Albert at one stage says to me: "The Hume/Adams report does not exist". And, now, they are at it again; Albert saying he never got it; Hume saying he gave it to Charlie Haughey, and I'll be interested in what, if anything, he [Haughey] has to say about it. I think Seamus Mallon once said he saw it, but, then, lots of people think they saw the Loch Ness monster. It may be better to suspend judgment until we see if the document is placed in the national archives.'

My last word on leaking: it operates on the basis that you're not actually leaking at all, even when you're whispering it down the phone to a salivating hack. The technique is quite simple: you tell the journalist something in the strictest confidence, just for his own information, deep background stuff, then sit back and confidently wait for him to publish it. It's a kind of double whammy; you win both ways; you get it out on an exclusive basis, and you can also enjoy the luxury of afterwards accusing him of betraying your confidence.

But, finally, beware the worst type of leak, the one which the source does not deny and actually confirms. It means trouble: 3 July 1994—'Emily O'Reilly (who else!) has *Sunday Business Post* story headlined: "Spring ready to leave coalition". It's straight from the horse's mouth stuff. Significantly, Labour not denying the story ...' And the deadly clincher—27 July 1994: 'I'm told Fergus calmly told the programme managers' meeting that, yes, it was he who briefed Emily about bringing down the government.'

That's the unfixable leak. It is then almost time to say goodnight, Dick; to look around for the lifeboats, Albert; and to bid one and all, good-bye.

Cleraun Media Conferences

The papers in this volume were delivered at the 7th Cleraun Media Conference held in Dublin on 21-22 February 1998. The title of the conference was 'Whose truth is it anyway? Developing editorial values and policies in Irish media'. The contribution of those who chaired the conference sessions is gratefully acknowledged. They were:

HELEN CALLANAN
Deputy Editor of the *Sunday Tribune*

SENATOR JOHN DARDIS
Deputy Leader of the Seanad, and correspondent with the *Irish Farmers' Journal*

DAMIEN KIBERD
Editor of the *Sunday Business Post*

JOE LITTLE
Religious and social affairs correspondent, RTE

RORY GODSON
Ireland Editor of the *Sunday Times*

MARIE McGONAGLE
Lecturer in law, National University of Ireland, Galway

PETER MOONEY
Producer, *Soundbyte*, RTE Radio 1

SENATOR SHANE ROSS
Business Editor of the *Sunday Independent*

DAVID QUINN
Editor of the *Irish Catholic*, and columnist with the *Sunday Times*

Also gratefully acknowledged is the help received from André Raynouard and Martine Moreau of the French Embassy in Dublin, from Stephen Ryan, editorial and design consultant with the *Irish Times*, and from Maurice Sweeney, design editor of the *Sunday Tribune* at the time of the conference.

Previous Cleraun Media Conferences have looked at a broad range of topics including:

- the role of media practitioners in society
- public service broadcasting and democracy
- the dangers posed by new media monopolies
- proposals to create a greater diversity in media
- ethical issues in news reporting, coverage of conflict, and advertising
- the media on terrorism, violence and crime
- the role of the media in the Northern Ireland peace process
- the use of broadcasting bans by government
- opening access to the airwaves and community radio
- investigative journalism
- Church-media relations
- regional versus national press
- media education
- ethical standards in the US, British and French media.

The proceedings of the 6th Cleraun Media Conference were also published by Open Air in *Media in Ireland. The Search for Diversity* (1997), now in its second printing.

The conferences are held in Cleraun at 90 Foster Avenue, Mount Merrion, Co. Dublin—a study centre and hall of residence for third level students which is an apostolic undertaking of Opus Dei, a prelature of the Catholic Church.

Index